HERB
LESTER'S
LONDON
ADDRESS
BOOK

Published in 2017 by Herb Lester Associates Ltd

Herb Lester's London Address Book
Text © Herb Lester Associates Ltd 2017
Cover design by Matt Chase © Herb Lester Associates Ltd 2017

A CIP catalogue record for this book is available from the
British Library

ISBN: 978-1-910023-63-1

Printed and bound in the United Kingdom by The Westdale Press Ltd
Cover: Cocoon offset 100% recycled board
Pages: Cocoon offset 100% recycled paper

Herb Lester Associates Ltd are committed to printing and publishing in
the United Kingdom using 100% recycled materials wherever possible.

Herb Lester Associates Limited Reg. No 7183338

To see the full range of Herb Lester books, guides and products
visit herblester.com

HERB LESTER'S LONDON ADDRESS BOOK

Using this book

All details are correct at the time of writing, but we advise you to call before setting out on a long journey. Events move fast in the metropolis; we accept no responsibility for changes to opening hours or closures.

Admission prices are not listed, please check websites for details. Opening times listed as seasonal will change during the year.

FROM THE MOMENT WE PUBLISHED OUR FIRST
London guide in 2010, people asked us for advice. What's a good place to eat alone? Are there still any decent pubs in Soho? Where are good places to buy books? Records? Magazines?

We answered all of these questions, and many more, and in the process this address book was created. Time and time again we've returned to these places, and now we make them available to all because we feel everyone who lives in or visits London should know about them too.

Don't consider this a must-see list; the 280 entries that follow are simply very good at what they do. So whether you're looking to buy socks, eat a bacon sandwich, or see contemporary art, here's where we suggest you do it.

Herb Lester Associates
London, September 2017

EAT & DRINK

No tables?
➺ St. John
Maltby (p58)
is just a few
doors away.

40 MALTBY STREET

Informal surroundings and an
unpretentious approach belie the
exceptional quality of the food, which
is genuinely seasonal and made for
sharing. It also slips down particularly
well with a glass of wine. Handy then
that this vaulted space is shared with
natural wine specialist Gergovie,
whose wares are available by the glass
or bottle. Seating is at the bar or high
tables, if you can get it; arrive as early
as you dare, there are no reservations.

40 Maltby Street, SE1 3PA
Tel: 020 7237 9247
*Wed-Thu: 5.30pm-10pm; Fri: 12.30pm-2pm &
5.30pm-10pm; Sat: 11am-10pm*

ABENO TOO

Come here for okonomi-yaki, usually
described as a sort of Japanese
omelette, which is partially correct.
Prepared in front of diners who sit
around a U-shaped steel cooking
counter, okonomi-yaki include egg,
cabbage, spring onions and pickled
ginger, with a variety of fillings, all of
which is then fried and slathered in

sauce. Somehow it still manages to look elegant, but be warned that since you're essentially eating in a kitchen, your clothes may hold the aroma of cooking long after your last bite.

17-18 Great Newport Street, WC2H 7JE
Tel: 020 7379 1160
Sun-Mon: 12noon-10pm;
Tue-Thu: 12noon-10.30pm;
Fri-Sat: 12noon-11pm

AMERICAN BAR AT THE SAVOY

Cocktail bars come and cocktail bars go, but the American Bar is forever. Fantastically glamorous and fantastically expensive, it's just as well that the cocktails are fantastic too. Which is no more than one would expect from a bar that's been at the summit of mixology for more than a century. Dress properly, as Noel Coward, Fred Astaire, Audrey Hepburn, Marlene Dietrich and countless others have done before you.

The Savoy, Strand, WC2R 0EU
Tel: 020 7836 4343
Mon-Sat: 11.30am-12midnight;
Sun: 12noon-12midnight

If you're still dressed up and need somewhere else to go
➻ Bar Américain at Brasserie Zédel, p18
➻ Dukes Bar, p27
➻ Upstairs at Rules, p55

ANDREW EDMUNDS

Ask a local where to go for a night of wooing and the odds are that here is where they'll point you. Occupying two floors of a dark Georgian house, it has a daily changing, handwritten menu of classic dishes and a highly praised wine list. Candlelight softens features and encourages lingering over one more drink. The pleasingly creaky place's aphrodisiac qualities may be overstated by some, but its intimate atmosphere can't be denied.

46 Lexington Street, W1F 0LP
Tel: 020 7437 5708
Mon-Fri: 12noon–3.30pm & 5.30pm-10.45pm;
Sat: 12.30pm-3.30pm & 5.30pm-10.45pm;
Sun: 1pm-4pm & 6pm-10.30pm

ASAKUSA

The shabby exterior is not going to lure many passers-by, fortunate then that this authentic Japanese restaurant has no need of them. The quality of the food and congenial atmosphere guarantees a full house every night, making booking essential – we suggest requesting a table upstairs or, for two, the counter.

265 Eversholt Street, NW1 1BA
Tel: 020 7388 8533
Mon-Sat: 6pm-11.30pm

BALTHAZAR BOULANGERIE

This Franco-American brasserie has quickly
become a favourite on the city's food scene,
but ignore at your peril the adjacent bakery.
A stylised reproduction of a classic boulangerie,
with gilded glass writing on the windows and
rows of rustic loaves bearing a capitalised italic
'B'. The traditional French breads and brioches
are what puts Balthazar in our book, but there
are also Viennoisserie and patisserie available to
take away.

4-6 Russell Street, WC2B 5HZ
Tel: 020 3301 1155
Mon-Fri; 8am-7.30pm; Sat: 9am-7.30pm; Sun: 9am-6pm

BAO BAR

You will need to be exceptionally lucky to get a
seat here without queuing, but the consensus
is that it's worth the wait. Bao – fluffy steamed
buns filled with fried chicken, lamb shoulder
and other delicacies – are the titular star of
this little Taiwanese restaurant, but other small
plates are also delicious.

53 Lexington Street, W1F 9AS
No phone
Mon-Wed: 12noon-3pm & 5.30pm-10pm;
Thu-Fri: 12noon-3pm & 5.30pm-10.30pm;
Sat: 12noon-10.30pm

BAR ITALIA

Just being open throughout the night is enough
to recommend it, but there's so much more.
The last survivor of London's post-war coffee
bar boom, and still run by the Polledri family
who opened it in 1949. Photos of the Italian
national football team on the walls are updated
and the TV is new; the moderne counter,
terrazzo floor, and many of its regulars are as
authentically old Soho as it gets.

22 Frith Street, W1D 4RF
Tel: 020 7437 4520
Daily: 24 hours

BAR REMO

Located seconds from Oxford Circus, this is an
example of a type of old-style Italian restaurant
that was once so prevalent in the West End and
is now all but extinct. For anyone trying to avoid
prying eyes, visit the large downstairs room
which, given the restaurant's proximity to the
former Decca Records press office and Great
Marlborough Street magistrate's courts, seems
almost to echo with intrigue.

2 Princes Street, W1B 2LB
Tel: 020 7629 1715
Mon-Fri: 10am-11pm; Sat: 12noon-11pm;
Sun: 12noon-10.30pm

THE BARBARY

The name refers to the Barbary Coast, which runs pretty much from modern day North Africa to the Middle East, and it's from there that the menu draws its inspiration. It's a mixture of familiar items perfectly rendered (fattoush, baba ghanoush) with dishes that staff may grow tired of explaining (chicken abu kalmash, octopus mashawsha), all of it fragrant and intense with spice. It's a tiny restaurant with seating for just 24, arranged in a semi-circle around an open kitchen; that means groups of more than four are a challenge and a wait is likely, but to pass the time with a drink in Neal's Yard is no hardship, and the meal is worth it.

No tables?
➡ Homeslice (p35) is almost next door in Neal's Yard.

16 Neal's Yard, WC2H 9DP
No phone, reservations for tables at 12noon and 5pm only, via thebarbary.co.uk
Mon-Fri: 12noon-3pm & 5pm-10pm;
Sat: 12noon-10pm; Sun: 12noon-9.30pm

**If you can't
stand the heat**
➻ Just across the
road, Barshu
has a sister
restaurant,
Bashan (24
Romilly Street,
W1D 5AH), that
serves Hunanese
food – lighter and
less fiery than
Szechuan
cooking.

BARSHU

One of the city's few Szechuan
specialists, with all the associated
flavourful intensity. Despite dishes
with names such as Numbing And
Hot Dried Beef, not everything on the
menu is blisteringly hot – although
the chilli-averse are advised to
order carefully. It's dark and serene,
decorated in rich shades of red and
yellow and elaborate carved wood,
with none of the rush and chaos that's
associated with restaurants just a few
steps away in Chinatown, on the other
side of Shaftesbury Avenue.

28 Frith Street, WID 5LF
Tel: 020 7287 8822
*Sun-Thu: 12noon-11pm;
Fri-Sat: 12noon-11.30pm*

BEPPE'S CAFE

Gloriously unreconstructed Anglo-
Italian caff close to Smithfield meat
market, frequented by cab drivers and
hospital workers from nearby Barts. Its
popularity lies not just in home-cooked
food (English breakfast, pasta dishes,
exemplary sandwiches) that's as tasty

as the portions are generous but also in its handsome appearance: mid-century signage, beaten-copper counter and comfortable red leatherette booths.

23 West Smithfield, EC1A 9HY
Tel: 020 7236 7822
Mon-Fri: 6.30am-3pm; Sat: 7am-1pm

BERBER & Q

Small groups are best placed to enjoy sharing smoked, charcoal-grilled meats served on boards with pickles, bread and salad. Vegetarians shouldn't give up, smoked aubergine imam bayildi and cauliflower shawarma are just two meat-free highlights. Excellent cocktails and ales from Morocco, Lebanon and Israel go some way to mitigate against the backdrop of high-decibel dance music which can be overwhelming at times. Reservations only for groups of four to 12.

Arch 338 Acton Mews, E8 4EA
Tel: 020 7923 0829
Tues-Fri: 6pm-11pm; Sat-Sun: 11am-11pm

Check out
some other
favourite Soho
drinking dens
➤➤ The Coach &
Horses, p23
➤➤ The French
House, p32
➤➤ The New
Evaristo, p48

THE BLUE POSTS

A blissfully unremarkable corner pub – even the name is commonplace, there are two more Blue Posts in Soho alone – it is still frequented by market traders from nearby Berwick Street, film and music business hustlers and strivers, and the occasional weary tourist. It has the worn-in living-room atmosphere familiar from the years before leather sofas and artfully mismatched armchairs took hold. Service is brisk, eavesdropping can be rewarding. For a quiet mid-afternoon reviver, it's all you can ask for.

22 Berwick Street W1F 0QA
Tel: 020 7437 5008
Mon-Thu: 11am-11pm;
Fri-Sat: 11am-12midnight;
Sun: 11am-11.30pm

BREDDOS TACOS

Simple street food is elevated to new heights at this small, informal taqueria – a modest but significant step up from food truck roots. Mexico is the primary inspiration, but influences come from all over, with kung pao chicken and

Sichuan octopus as toppings on the housemade tacos, tostadas and tlayudas (large, baked tortillas).

82 Goswell Road, EC1V 7DB
Tel: 020 3535 8301
Mon-Sat: 12noon-3pm & 5pm-11pm;
Sun: 11am-6pm

BOB BOB RICARD

Enjoy a taste of how it feels to be rich and spoiled in this wildly over-the-top restaurant that looks like a Versace-Wes Anderson collaboration. There's booth seating throughout, each equipped with a button to press for a champagne delivery. If that sounds too showy to be comfortable, it's not. It's surprisingly cosy in a cocoon-like way, with flattering lighting, attentive staff and Russian-inspired food that may not be cheap but at least it's excellent.

1 Upper James Street, W1F 9DF
Tel: 020 3145 1000
Sun-Wed: 12.30pm-3pm & 6pm-12midnight;
Thu-Sat: 12.30pm-3pm & 5.30pm-1am

Five more suggestions for a louche night
➺ American Bar at The Savoy, p9
➺ Duck & Waffle, p26
➺ Dukes, p27
➺ Randall & Aubin, p52
➺ Yauatcha, p62

More brasserie-style options
➺ Balthazar, p11
➺ Fischer's, p30
➺ Hoi Polloi, p34

BRASSERIE ZÉDEL

A magnifcently restored Art Deco delight beneath the West End streets. The main dining room is vast, with a relaxing hum of conversation and flattering light. Linen table cloths, efficient staff and French brasserie classics all feel expensive, but it can be extraordinary value – the two-course prix fixe is £9.75. At busy times, lingering is discouraged, which can necessitate a trip to the lovely Bar Américain for cocktails. A café at street level is pleasant but lacks the drama on offer below ground.

20 Sherwood Street, W1F 7ED
Tel: 020 7734 4888
Brasserie, Mon-Sat: 11.30am-12midnight;
Sun: 11.30am-11pm
Bar Américain, Mon-Wed: 4.30pm-12midnight;
Thu-Fri: 4.30pm-1am; Sat: 1pm-1am;
Sun: 4.30pm-11pm
Café, Mon-Fri: 8am-11pm; Sat: 9am-11pm;
Sun: 11.30am-11pm

THE BULL AND LAST

Conveniently located for Hampstead Heath, on the ground floor, the dark, woody feel of a traditional pub has been carefully maintained. Next to the bar an open kitchen turns out excellent modern European food and Sunday lunches that are a reminder of just how good a roast can be. The first floor restaurant has the same menu in a slightly more formal setting.

168 Highgate Road, NW5 1QS
Tel: 020 7267 3641
Mon-Thu: 12noon-11pm;
Fri: 12noon-12midnight;
Sat: 9am-12midnight; Sun: 9am-10.30pm

BÚNBÚNBÚN

There are well over a dozen Vietnamese restaurants on Kingsland Road, so it takes something to stand out. This newish arrival specialises in bún (noodle salads, thick with fresh herbs, topped with grilled meat, fish or tofu) but salt and chilli soft shell crab, prawns, squid, ribs and tofu are noteworthy, and £10 set meals are excellent value for the solo diner. It's a small space that affects a pared back modern look – school chairs, bare bulbs, rough plaster walls – with diners crammed in a little too tightly for privacy at peak times.

134B Kingsland Road, E2 8DY
Tel: 020 7729 6494
Daily: 12noon-11pm

CAMPANIA GASTRONOMIA

Coffee, eggs, pastries and sourdough toast in the morning through to a full Southern Italian menu in the evening. The smell of cooking garlic from about 11am is enough to make anyone walking past start to think about lunch way too early. Located in the former Jones Dairy, just off Columbia Road, it has a few outside tables, an open air courtyard and seating indoors for small and large groups.

23 Ezra Street, E2 7RH
Tel: 020 7613 0015
Tue-Fri: 8.30am-3.30pm & 7pm-11pm;
Sat: 10am-5pm & 7pm-11pm; Sun: 9am-6pm

CAPRINI

Traditional Italian restaurant of the breadstick and chianti variety. Old-fashioned décor and service make this feel like an outpost from a different time, as does unchallenging, comforting food. Take note of the fascia, with its optimistic serif type and sweet tilework depicting a couple enjoying a meal under an umbrella, oblivious to the traffic roaring south from Waterloo Bridge.

77 Waterloo Road, SE1 8UD
Tel: 020 7928 6645
Mon-Fri: 12noon-3pm & 5pm-11.30pm;
Sat: 12noon-11.30pm; Sun: 12noon-11pm

CARAVAN

Relaxed all-day dining with items to suit most appetites: snacks, small plates and full meals that draw inspiration from all over, notably the Far and Middle East. Housed in what was a Victorian grain store, adjoining the new home of Central Saint Martins art school, it's a huge space that feels both lively and intimate.

1 Granary Building, Granary Square, N1C 4AA
Tel: 020 7101 7661
Mon-Fri: 8am-10.30pm; Sat: 10am-10.30pm;
Sun: 10am-4pm

THE CARPENTER'S ARMS

Small, sensitively renovated pub a short walk from Brick Lane, that achieves a balance of East End old and new. Good ales and food, and a location that's just far enough off the beaten track for everyone's comfort. The small beer garden is a rare treat for the area and an added incentive to visit – if such a thing were needed.

73 Cheshire Street, E2 6EG
Tel: 020 7739 6342
Mon-Wed: 4pm-11.30pm; Thu: 12noon-11.30pm;
Fri-Sat: 12noon-12.30am; Sun: 12noon-11.30pm

Other branches
➻ 11-13 Exmouth Market, EC1R 4QD
➻ 30 Great Guildford Street, SE1 0HS
➻ Bloomberg Arcade, 3 Queen Victoria Street, EC2R

CIAO BELLA

Eternally popular, always busy Italian restaurant that's as notable for exuberant atmosphere as reliable food – spaghetti al cartoccio, seafood in tomato sauce cooked inside a paper bag is a standout. Across the board appeal is a large part of its charm, drawing locals and tourists from a wide spectrum to its tightly packed dining room and outdoor seating on pedestrianised Lamb's Conduit Street.

86-90 Lamb's Conduit Street, WC1N 3LZ
Tel: 020 7242 4119
Mon-Sat: 12noon-11.30pm; Sun: 12noon-10.30pm

THE CITTIE OF YORKE

There are numerous reasons to visit this historic pub, not least to see its wonderful vaulted ceiling and smokeless fireplace. Those wishing to converse unheard should make their way to the rear bar (through one of two entrances) where ornate wooden booths are purpose-built for just such an exchange.

22 High Holborn, WC1V 6BN
Tel: 020 7242 7670
Mon-Sat: 12noon-11pm

THE CLOVE CLUB

Impeccable modern cooking that makes use of the finest available ingredients, served from an open kitchen in a dining room that does little to hide its municipal history. All of which is nothing like as austere as it sounds. Servers bring the enthusiasm of a private host, and set tasting menus are a masterclass in dish pairing – and terrific fun to eat.

Shoreditch Town Hall, 380 Old Street, EC1V 9LT
Tel: 020 7729 6496
Mon: 6pm-9pm; Tue-Sat: 12noon-2pm & 6pm-9pm

THE COACH & HORSES

Perhaps Soho's most famous hostelry, it remains a favourite of locals as well as visitors eager to see where Jeffrey Bernard, Francis Bacon and other West End notables and undesirables spent so much of their time. Its interior is unpretentious, a pleasing blend of wood and red Formica, with authentic 1970s touches. It is perhaps at its best on Sundays; during the day it is peaceful and quiet, come the evening a cheerful sing-along begins.

29 Greek Street, W1D 5DH
Tel: 020 7437 5920
Mon-Thu: 11am-11.30pm; Fri & Sat: 11am-12midnight;
Sun: 12noon-11pm

Don't drink on an empty stomach!
➻ Get ramen at Kanada-Ya (p38), just a short walk from here

THE CROSS KEYS

Easily spotted by a proud display of foliage and drinkers spilling into the street, its exterior charm is considerable, but it's even better inside. One of the most dimly lit pubs we know, rose-coloured bulbs provide a warm glow and just enough light to make out the eccentric assemblage hanging from walls and ceiling: copper pots and kettles, an old diver's helmet, photographs and paintings. A comfortable place with friendly bar staff and Brodie's excellent ales; it feels a long way from the madness of Covent Garden just a few feet away.

31 Endell Street, WC2H 9BA
Tel: 020 7836 5185
Mon-Sat: 11am-11pm; Sun: 12noon-10.30pm

DEHESA

Shoppers weary of Regent Street may wish to restore themselves here with a quick glass of wine and plate of cheese or charcuterie, or one can linger for several hours over small plates of Spanish and Italian-inspired tapas. It's small and can get busy, but think

of it instead as lively and intimate.
Beware, the bill can soon add up,
helped by an excellent selection of
wines by the glass.

Kingly Court, 25 Ganton Street, W1F 9BP
Tel: 020 7494 4170
Mon-Fri: 12noon-3pm & 5pm-11pm;
Sat: 10am-11pm; Sun: 10am-10pm

DISHOOM

Merging Indian food with all-day
brasserie-style dining is an inspired
concept. That cleverness extends to
meticulously designed spaces, with
each location recalling a different
aspect of Bombay's past. Consistently
excellent food is intense in flavour
without being overpowering or heavy
– the black daal is particularly good.
Lunch and evenings are busiest, so
try to make time for breakfast of
bacon and egg naan roll or fried eggs
on chilli cheese toast.

12 Upper St. Martin's Lane, WC2H 9FB
Tel: 020 7420 9320
Mon-Thu: 8am-11pm; Fri: 8am-12midnight;
Sat: 9am-12midnight; Sun: 9am-11pm

Other branches
➡ 7 Boundary
Street, E2 7JE
➡ 5 Stable
Street, N1C 4AB
➡ 22 Kingly
Street, W1B 5QP

Four more South Asian favourites
➥ Dishoom, p25
➥ India Club at The Hotel Strand Continental, p36
➥ Roti King, p54
➥ Tayyabs, p61

DIWANA BHEL POORI HOUSE

The unassuming elder statesman of London Indian restaurants since the 1960s. It is entirely unselfconscious, with hard benches, stainless steel beakers and trays and a vegetarian menu. The lunchtime buffet (Mon-Fri: 12noon-2.30pm; Sat-Sun: 12noon-4pm) is far from the pea and potato gloop of similar establishments; salads, curries, homemade pickles and chutneys are all freshly made and constantly refreshed. It is one of the city's great food bargains, attracting nearby office workers, impecunious pensioners, weary travelers and plenty of regulars. 'A la carte' bhel poori and dosas are also excellent.

121-123 Drummond Street, NW1 2HL
Tel: 020 7387 5556
Mon-Sat: 12noon-11.30pm;
Sun: 12noon-10.30pm

DUCK & WAFFLE

One of the best views of the city and open 24 hours? That's a double USP. Add great, indulgent food that's not insanely priced (the signature duck leg confit with fried duck egg is £17; parmesan and truffle polenta bites £3 each), and we confess that this is one shining new tower we can live with. Window seats are sought after, but even if all are taken, everyone can enjoy the view from the rocket-powered lift that goes from ground to the 40th floor in a matter of seconds.

40th Floor, 110 Bishopsgate, EC2N 4AY
Tel: 020 3640 7310
Daily: 24 hours

DUKES BAR

Ian Fleming's bar of choice is discreet and comfortable in a quiet cul-de-sac off St James's. It's a grown-up sort of place for grown-up drinks. A Bond-inspired martini is created from freezer-cold spirits wheeled on a trolley to your table and served with minimal fuss. No one here will thank you for requesting your martini shaken not stirred, but it wouldn't be the first time they'd heard it. Sloppy clothes on the other hand – and that includes trainers and sportswear – will not be tolerated.

Dukes Hotel, 35 St James's Place, SW1A 1NY
Tel: 020 7491 4840
Mon-Sat: 2pm-11pm; Sun: 4pm-10.30pm

E PELLICCI

With its Art Deco wood interior and cheering neon fan signage, there can be no more beautiful café in the country than this. For all its reputation as a hangout for the East End's most illustrious and infamous residents (Gilbert and George, Idris Elba, Ray Winstone and at one time, the Kray Twins), Pellicci has no airs, it is warm and friendly with comforting, homemade Anglo-Italian food to match.

332 Bethnal Green Road, E2 0AG
Tel: 020 7739 4873
Mon-Sat: 7am-4pm

THE EAGLE

In all likelihood the first ever gastropub, serving excellent, unpretentious food and good drinks since 1991. Despite the open kitchen it's still very much a pub, in which drinkers and eaters mingle happily. Orders are taken at the bar, there are no tablecloths, no waiters and prices are reasonable. The chalkboard menu changes regularly, but a steak sandwich is usually available and always terrific.

159 Farringdon Road, EC1R 3AL
Tel: 020 7837 1353
Mon-Fri: 12noon-3pm & 6.30pm-10.30pm; Sat: 12.30pm-3.30pm & 6.30pm-10.30pm; Sun: 12.30pm-4pm

EL PARADOR

Tapas are fresh and inexpensive, and the atmosphere convivial at this family-run Spanish restaurant, its modest appearance belying the quality of the food. On summer nights, the prime spot is the back garden, a leafy oasis in this sooty stretch of Mornington Crescent. Empty tables are rare, so booking is advised.

245 Eversholt Street, NW1 1BA
Tel: 020 7387 2789
Mon-Fri: 12noon-3pm; Mon-Thu: 6am-11pm;
Fri-Sat: 6pm-11.30pm; Sun: 6.30pm-9.30pm

EL PASTOR

One of the new breed of Mexican restaurants righting the wrongs perpetuated in the name of that country's food. Brick walls, bare bulbs and corrugated iron suit the fresh, punchy flavours that come from the kitchen. Of the excellent tacos, most notable is the Al Pastór, with its 24-hour marinated pork shoulder. Splendid cocktails and a large mezcal list enhance the exuberant atmosphere. No reservations, but they'll text when a table is ready, allowing you to wander the bars of adjacent Borough Market.

7a Stoney Street, SE1 9AA
No phone
Mon-Sat: 12noon-3pm & 6pm-11pm

FINO'S WINE CELLAR

Devour pizza and guzzle Valpolicella in the alcoves of this 1980s timewarp wine bar and restaurant deep in Mayfair. Very much hidden in plain sight, Fino's old-fashioned charm draws loyal regulars and a smattering of tourists who happen upon it.

123 Mount Street, W1K 3NP
Tel: 020 7491 1640
Mon-Fri: 12noon-3pm & 6pm-10.45pm
Bar open all day

FISCHER'S

Without a spoilsport to tell you otherwise, you might think this a leftover from another era, so well realised is the 1920s Mitteleuropean fantasy spun by Chris Corbin and Jeremy King, also of Brasserie Zédel (p18), The Wolseley, The Delaunay, et al. For breakfast you may have gröstl – a hash of paprika, potato, egg and bacon; served throughout the day are schnitzels, würstchen, brötchen and, of course, konditorei (don't miss the poppy seed cake), hot chocolate and coffee. It's delicious, comfortable and very hard to leave.

50 Marylebone High Street, W1U 5HN
Tel: 020 7466 5501
Mon-Sat: 7.30am-11pm; Sun: 8am-10.30pm

FOUR SEASONS

It's better to do one thing well than many things adequately. At the Four Seasons that thing is roast duck. Many say it's the best in Chinatown, others that it's the best in London; a few claim it has no rival anywhere. We'll just say it's very good indeed. A full menu is available, but let us make this very clear: order the roast duck.

12 Gerrard Street, W1D 5PR
Tel: 020 7494 0870
Mon-Thu: 12noon-11:30pm ;
Fri-Sat: 12noon-12midnight; Sun: 11am-11pm

Other branches
➤➤ 4 Queensway,
W2 3RL

FRANZE & EVANS

Surprisingly unheralded café/ restaurant that serves wonderful food throughout the day. Service can be a little fractious, but this is a minor inconvenience when weighed against a range of wonderful salads in the Ottolenghi vein, or a croissant with honey, thyme and goat's cheese.

101 Redchurch Street, E2 7DL
Tel: 020 7033 1910
Mon-Wed: 8am-7pm; Thu-Fri: 8am-11pm;
Sat: 9am-11pm; Sun: 9.30am-7pm

THE FRENCH HOUSE

There may be no other pub in the land that will reject a customer's simple request for a pint, but here at The French they don't believe in them, nor will they countenance ale. Only lager, French cider, wines and spirits are available here, yet we love it still. Writing in 1966, Frank Norman said that 'today the drinkers in the French Pub are rather different from those of long ago, but it is still packed with advertising men, actors, a few writers, one or two bums and a great many ordinary people who have popped in for a glass of beer during their lunch hour, and there is never much elbow room.' We are delighted to confirm that this holds true today.

49 Dean Street, W1D 5BG
Tel: 020 7437 2477/2799
Mon-Sat: 12noon-11pm; Sun: 12noon-10.30pm

FRYER'S DELIGHT

Unpretentious, authentic fish and chip shop, beloved of cabbies and the Old Bill, whose station is opposite. Take away is an option but you'd be a fool to not make time to enjoy the interior, still decked out in shades of Formica.

19 Theobalds Road, WC1X 8SL
Tel: 020 7405 4114
Mon-Sat: 12noon-10.30pm

GELATORINO

There are prettier places for gelato, but a cup of fiordilatte (made of sweetened cream with no flavouring) eaten with a little coloured spoon is as delicious and authentically Italian an experience as any available in this city.

2 Russell Street, WC2B 5JD
Tel: 020 7240 0746
Mon-Thu: 12noon-8pm; Fri-Sat: 11am-10.30pm;
Sun: 12noon-8pm

GEORGE BAR AT DURRANTS HOTEL

Resolutely old-fashioned, comfortable bar that comes into its own in the winter months. Comfortable chairs, a coal fire, the clink of ice into glasses and hushed conversation. It feels almost as much a refuge from the modern world as it is from the busy streets of Marylebone. The same can be said for the hotel as a whole, a terrace of four Georgian houses knocked into one, run by the Miller family since the 1920s with an air of discreet professionalism.

26-32 George Street, W1H 5BJ
Tel: 020 7935 8131
Daily: 11am-11pm

GORDON'S WINE BAR

On the incline that leads to Embankment tube and the Thames, this candle-lit wine bar feels almost carved out of the riverbank. Dark, cosy and intimate, it's a popular spot for courting couples as well as those lured by the substantial range of wine by the glass and bottle.

47 Villiers Street, WC2N 6NE
Tel: 020 7930 1408
Mon-Sat: 11am-11pm; Sun: 12noon-10pm

H T HARRIS

Family-run Italian sandwich and snack bar that specialises in toasted ciabatta sandwiches. Lightly charred on the outside and loaded with fresh ingredients of your choice, they are crisp and delicious, a far cry from the ubiquitous soggy panini. On a chilly day, soup or pasta is a comforting option.

41 Great Titchfield Street, W1W 7PG
Tel: 020 7636 4228
Mon-Fri: 7am-6pm; Sat: 8am-4pm

HOI POLLOI

In an area that's full of small, no-booking restaurants, here's one where you can almost always find a table, regardless of whether you feel like three courses, brunch or a snack –

handy if you've just booked in at the adjacent
Ace Hotel and don't know if it's morning or
night. Entered via a flower shop, it's a large
room with blonde wood panelling, honeycomb
tiles, pink walls and a variety of seating from
tables to comfortable booths.

Ace Hotel, 100 Shoreditch High Street, E1 6JQ
Tel: 020 8880 6100
Daily: 7am-12midnight

HOMESLICE

Pizza, beer and wine sounds like a recipe for
a party, and that's pretty much how it is here.
Communal seating and paper plates create
an informal environment and hefty 20-inch
sourdough pizzas are made for sharing. In
the fiercely contested pizza arena, these are
among the very best, both in the pure form of
margherita or with a more adventurous topping
such as goat shoulder, savoy cabbage and sumac
yoghurt. Individual slices are available, but a
whole pie is the wiser choice.There are two
additional outlets at the time of writing, in
Fitzrovia and Shoreditch.

13 Neal's Yard, WC2H 9DP
Tel: 020 3151 7488
Daily: 12noon-11pm

HONEY & CO

Sophisticated yet unfussy Levantine food from an ex-Ottolenghi husband and wife team who bring a familial warmth to the proceedings. Weekend breakfast is recommended, as is lunch and dinner – prompting the question, is three times too often to visit in a single day? Deservedly busy, but counter seats are kept open for walk-ins.

25A Warren Street, W1T 5LZ
Tel: 020 7388 6175
Mon-Fri: 8am-10:30pm; Sat: 9.30am-10.30pm

INDIA CLUB AT THE HOTEL STRAND CONTINENTAL

Enter through a small doorway next to a convenience store and up a narrow staircase. In addition to discreet lodgings, this budget hotel is home to the 70-year-old India Club, with a light and airy bar on the first floor. Hearty, modestly-priced Indian food is available in the restaurant, up one more flight of stairs. A true time warp, with polite staff, fair prices, and a pleasantly lived-in atmosphere. It is probably as close to (Graham) Greeneland as we are likely to find in central London at this late date.

143 The Strand, WC2R 1JA
Tel: 020 7836 4880
Daily: 12noon-2.30pm & 6pm-10.50pm

THE JERUSALEM TAVERN

Bad weather has its benefits, and an excuse to hole up here is one of them. Warm and snug, with open fires, creaking wood floors and the full range of St Peter's ales, there are few cosier spots in London. Despite appearances, it's a relatively new pub, an artful 1990s recreation of something far older, albeit in a genuine 18th-century building.

55 Britton Street, EC1M 5UQ
Tel: 020 7490 4281
Mon-Fri: 11am-11pm

JOE ALLEN

A theatreland favourite since 1977. Though it's recently changed owners and moved a short distance, were a patron to turn up after a few years' absence they'd discern little difference: brick walls, show posters, flattering light, maybe even a few old faces. It's a place loved for its atmosphere rather than showy cooking – black bean soup, buffalo wings, Caesar salad, steaks, and an off-menu burger that may be the worst-kept secret in London.

2 Burleigh Street, WC2E 7PX
Tel: 020 7836 0651
Mon-Thu: 8am-11.30pm; Fri: 8am-12.30am;
Sat: 9am-12.30am; Sun: 9am-10.30pm

JOSÉ

This corner tapas bar is always busy – even weekday lunchtimes can be a crush. But this is the sort of food that was meant to be eaten on the fly, so stand at the bar with a glass of sherry and enjoy a snack while watching chefs carve meats and prepare plates.

104 Bermondsey Street, SE1 3UB
Tel: 020 7403 4902
Mon-Sat: 12noon-10.15pm; Sun: 12noon-5.15pm

KANADA-YA

Other branches
➼ 3 Panton Street, SW1Y 4DL

Occupying a cute corner site in St Giles, this transplant from Kyushu, Japan, serves a particularly good tonkotsu ramen that's rich, silky and, unfortunately for vegetarians, made from pork bones. It's a small space with shared tables and the strong chance of a queue, but the simple menu makes ordering fast and diners tend not to linger. A second branch near Haymarket is larger, with reservations available.

64 St Giles High Street, WC2H 8LE
Tel: 020 7240 0232
Mon-Sat: 12noon-3pm & 5pm-10.30pm

KÊU

No matter how good the filling may be, a sandwich is only as good as the bread used to make it. Nowhere is this more true than in the Franco-Viet bánh mì, where a baguette, filled with meat, pickled vegetables, chilli and sauce, has to yield to the bite without losing its crunch. Kêu have their bread made to order, resulting in a perfectly crisp sandwich that's never doughy or soggy. The menu extends to other Vietnamese street food, but the bánh mì is where it's at.

332 Old Street, EC1V 9DR
Tel: 020 7739 1164
Mon-Sat: 9am-9pm

THE KING CHARLES I

Despite its location in the transient backstreets of Kings Cross, there's the feeling here of being in a proper local. Small, wood-panelled and littered with taxidermy, masks and old signs, it has a most convivial atmosphere. All of which is conducive to ordering just one more for the road – so be warned if you have a train to catch.

55-57 Northdown Street, N1 9BL
Tel: 020 7837 7758
Mon-Tue: 5pm-11pm; Wed-Fri: 12noon-12midnight;
Sat: 5pm-11pm; Sun: 5pm-10.30pm

Five more
recommendations
for the solo diner
➜ E Pellici, p28
➜ Honey & Co,
p36
➜ Padella, p49
➜ Paul Rothe,
p50
➜ Taro, p60

KOYA BAR

There's only counter seating at this little Japanese restaurant, all of it arranged around the orderly open kitchen, making it an ideal place to dine alone or in a pair – which is just as well because snagging even one of the 25 seats can be hard enough. Congee and cold noodles are available for breakfast, still an uncommon sight in London, and there's also a Japanese take on the Full English too. Cultural crossover is seen again with a version of fish and chips; udon noodles, seaweed, tofu and other classic dishes are all excellent too.

50 Frith Street, W1D 4SQ
No phone
Mon-Wed: 8.30am-10.30pm;
Thu-Fri: 8.30am-11pm;
Sat: 9.30am-11pm; Sun: 9.30am-10pm

LEILA'S CAFÉ / SHOP

Simple food made from excellent ingredients: sandwiches of comte cheese, eggs and serrano ham, lentil soup with spinach, maybe a lump of chocolate or an orange afterwards.

Bread and butter is particularly noteworthy. Their shop next door sells loose pulses, grains and coffee, cheese, ham and a small, fragrant selection of fruit, vegetables and herbs.

15-17 Calvert Avenue, E2 7JP
Tel: 020 7729 9789
Wed-Sat: 10am-6pm: Sun: 10am-5pm

LOBOS MEAT & TAPAS

Hungry like the wolf? This restaurant will fulfil most carnivorous cravings, with a particular emphasis on Iberico pork. Spanish food is well represented in this neck of the woods, so consider this a younger, wilder sibling of José and Brindisa. The tunnel-like space is dark and fashionably rough around the edges and the music loud. Not a place for the sheepish.

14 Borough High Street, SE1 9QG
Tel: 020 7407 5361
Mon-Fri: 12noon-3.30pm & 5.30pm-11pm;
Sat: 12noon-4pm & 5.30pm-11pm;
Sun: 12noon-4pm & 5.30pm-10pm

For more Borough tapas
➤ Brindisa at Borough Market, p124
➤ Jose, p38

LYLE'S

Restraint is the keyword: wooden chairs, white tiles, glass beakers. Menus eschew descriptions for a stark list of ingredients that offers no hint as to what the team labouring in the open kitchen has planned, but servers will gladly elaborate and also offer guidance through an unconventional wine list. There's rare skill at work here, in a style that nods in the direction of St. John in its affection for wild salad and bloody bits, albeit with a delicate touch. Note that evenings are set menu only, with an added vegetarian option.

56 Shoreditch High Street, E1 6JJ
Tel: 020 3011 5911
Mon-Sat: 12noon-2.30pm & 6pm-10pm

MAGGIE JONES'S

This cosy stalwart looks little changed in the last 40 or so years. Arranged over three floors, all awash in copper pots, baskets of dried flowers, enamel advertising signs and oak and pine furniture, Maggie Jones's is an oxymoron: both authentically 1970s and quite delicious. Food is a perfect match for the decor; classic British and a few French dishes, all expertly cooked and unpretentiously served, with not a thought for current trends. Come here for pies, roasts, pate, puddings and gallons of wine, preferably on a cold winter's night – just as Princess Margaret used to.

6 Old Court Place, Kensington Church Street, W8 4PL
Tel: 020 7937 6462
Mon-Sat: 12noon-2.30pm & 6pm-10.30pm;
Sun: 12noon-2.30pm & 6pm-10pm

MAISON BERTAUX

Striped blue and white awnings keep the sun off tempting displays of cakes and pastries in London's oldest French patisserie. Enjoy them to take away or in the charming, frilly tea room. For a very different atmosphere, place your order at the counter and ascend the steep, worn stairs to a room equipped with worn wood-effect tables and a selection of mismatched chairs. It's an environment that sounds utterly charmless but the effect is quite the opposite.

28 Greek Street, W1D 5DQ
Tel: 020 7437 6007
Mon-Sat: 8.30am-11pm; Sun: 8.30am-9pm

More Maltby Street highlights
➤➤ Gyoza Guys
➤➤ Herman Ze German
➤➤ Sub Cult
➤➤ The Modern Beer Bar

MALTBY STREET MARKET

Frequently linked with Druid Street and Borough Market because of proximity, the emphasis here is less on producers (although there are some) and more on street food. An atmospheric pedestrian street of railway arches with bunting and flags strewn across, it feels like a year-round street party with a bewildering number of eating and drinking options. These range from eat-as-you-walk, not so easy with a monster-sized sandwich spilling its filling, to permanent sites such as Little Bird Gin's bar, a recommended spot to people-watch. Note: bring cash, most stallholders won't take cards and there are few banks in the area.

Ropewalk, SE1 3PA
Sat: 9am-4pm; Sun: 11am-4pm

MANGAL 1 OCAKBASI

In an area brimming with fine Turkish food, Mangal 1 has long been the reigning champion. The formula is simple: grilled meat, homemade bread, salads, basic tables, warm service. And if that sounds easy to replicate, try any of the many unrelated restaurants with similar names to learn what rare alchemy is practiced here. Expect to queue, and to leave entirely sated. Note: alcohol is not served but drinkers are welcome to bring their own; corkage not charged.

10 Arcola Street, E8 2DJ
Tel: 020 7275 8981
Daily: 12noon-12midnight

More BYO
(Bring Your Own)
➻ India Club at The Hotel Strand Continental, p36
➻ Marie's, p45
➻ Rochelle Canteen, p53
➻ Roti King, p54
➻ Tayyabs, p61

MARIE'S

The sign over the door with its welcoming cuppa has enticed customers across the threshold for decades, and you can still get a lovely cup of tea here. These days the classic British menu is augmented with home-cooked Thai food, which means you can have liver and bacon or a cheese and pickle roll with a side of tom yum – until 5pm anyway, evenings are Thai only. The exceptional value and BYO policy can make it very busy.

90 Lower Marsh SE1 7AB
Tel: 020 7928 1050
Mon-Fri: 7am-10.30pm;
Sat: 7am-4pm & 5pm-10.30pm

THE MARKSMAN

From the street, it can still pass as a traditional Victorian boozer, but tables laid for dinner – and a Bib Gourmand award – tell another story. Food is hearty and exceptionally well done: pork belly with split peas; duck leg and turnips; chicken and wild garlic pie. And if mutton curry is on the menu, it's not to be missed. Should you object to paying restaurant prices to eat in a pub, upstairs there's a dining room with the bonus of banquette seating and a rather wonderful floor.

254 Hackney Road, E2 7SJ
Tel: 020 7739 7393
Mon-Fri: 11am-12midnight; Fri-Sat: 11am-1am;
Sun: 10am-11pm

MILKBAR

There's a touch of trompe l'oeil to the red, white and blue stripes on the door that look like a PVC strip curtain flapping in the breeze. That feeling of informality filters throughout this café which has all the qualities of its older sibling Flat White (17 Berwick Street, W1F 0PT) with the added benefit of more space.

3 Bateman Street, W1D 4AG
Tel: 020 7734 0370
Mon-Fri: 8am-5.30pm; Sat-Sun: 9.30am-6pm

MILROY'S OF SOHO

The city's oldest whisky shop has learned some new tricks. Now supplemented with a 12-seat bar, tasting area and below-ground cocktail bar, The Vault, reached through a false bookcase door. Dimly lit without being gloomy, here's a place to hole up in comfort while savouring knock-you-flat mixed drinks. For those who hate to drink alone, a private room is available for parties.

3 Greek Street, W1D 4NX
Tel: 020 7734 2277
Mon: 10am-7pm; Tue-Fri: 10am-12midnight

MORO

A convivial, noisy, stalwart that offers a distinctly British take on Spanish and North African cooking. Opened in the 1990s, before Exmouth Market was lined with bars and restaurants, it's been a model of consistency and excellence, despite a revolution in how and what we eat. From the charred yet moist bread and peppery olive oil to the last bite of their famous yoghurt cake, nothing about Moro disappoints.

34-36 Exmouth Market, EC1R 4QE
Tel: 020 7833 8336
Mon-Sat: 12pm-2.30pm & 6pm-10.30pm;
Sun: 12.30pm-2.45pm

THE NEW EVARISTO CLUB

From the mid-1940s until the early 2000s, this club's core clientele was of Italian and Spanish descent, taking a break from restaurant jobs in the surrounding streets. It's now a more open place, with cab drivers, fashion students, policemen and bemused tourists crammed into its confines.

57 Greek Street, W1D 3DX
Tel: 020 7437 9536
Daily: 5.30pm-1am

THE OLD BELL TAVERN

After the Great Fire, Sir Christopher Wren had this pub built for workers labouring on his reconstruction of neighbouring St Bride's Church. It has undergone extensive refurbishment over the years and Wren's builders have been replaced by printers, journalists and latterly office workers, but it's a pleasant place, particularly when it's warm enough to take drinks outside, facing the tranquil churchyard. Best approached via the passage to the side of St Bride's Church, which is directly behind.

95 Fleet Street EC4Y 1DH
Tel: 020 7583 0216
Mon-Fri: 11am-11pm; Sat: 12noon-8pm; Sun: 12noon-4pm

OTTOLENGHI

Global fame means queues are a feature of Yotam Ottolenghi's restaurants. Islington has long communal tables, with prepared dishes ordered from the counter served right away, hot items as they're ready. Spitalfields is arranged with a front section for takeaway and a separate dining room. Diners are never rushed and staff are ready with suggestions. Belgravia and Notting Hill branches, also recommended, are geared more towards takeaway.

287 Upper Street, N1 2TZ
Tel: 020 7288 1454
Mon-Sat: 8am-10.30pm; Sun: 9am-7pm

50 Artillery Lane, E1 7LJ
Tel: 020 7247 1999
Mon-Fri: 8am-10.30pm; Sat: 9am-10:30pm; Sun: 9am-6pm

PADELLA

Freshly made pasta is the thing here – and they make it exceptionally well, as seen in the open kitchen snugly encased by a marble counter at which diners perch. There are tables too, with additional seating downstairs, but expect to wait for whatever seat you need; there are no reservations and queues likely.

6 Southwark Street, SE1 1TQ
No phone
Mon-Sat: 12noon-4pm & 5pm-10pm; Sun: 12noon-5pm

PAUL ROTHE & SON

Opened in 1900 as a German delicatessen, this little sandwich shop exerts a spell. The counter and small dining area is manned by white-jacketed father and son, models of hospitality both, who take your order and prepare your food. A cup of coffee and a liverwurst sandwich makes for a nourishing and serene break in a hectic day.

36 Marylebone Lane, W1U 2NN
Tel: 020 7935 6783
Mon-Fri: 8am-6pm; Sat: 11am-5pm

POLPO

There are five branches of Polpo in London as of this writing, with several more around the country, but for all that expansion, this is a chain restaurant we keep going back to. The original Beak Street branch sets the tone for the others: small, crowded and lively, serving consistently delicious Venetian-style small plates (meatballs, fritto misto, arancini) at fair prices. It's almost always busy, so put your name on the list and head to the downstairs bar for an aperitivo.

41 Beak Street, W1F 9SB
Tel: 020 7734 4479
Mon-Thu: 8am-11pm; Fri: 8am-12midnight;
Sat: 11.30am-12midnight; Sun: 11.30am-10pm

THE PRIDE OF SPITALFIELDS

From the outside this looks like a country pub, but once inside it has no such rural charm. Clashing red carpet and worn burgundy seating dominate; it demands to be taken as is and, with its excellent real ale and a cat roaming unruffled among the tables, we are happy to do just that.

3 Heneage Street, E1 5LJ
Tel: 020 7247 8933
Mon-Thu: 10am-1am; Fri & Sat: 10am-2am;
Sun: 10am-12midnight

PRINCI

An informal, elegant import from Milan. It's split into areas of communal tables and counter service on the right, with table service and more substantial food on the left. It comes into its own for a mid-morning snack or last drink before the tube home.

135 Wardour Street, W1F 0UT
Tel: 020 7478 8886
Pizzeria, Mon-Sat: 8am-11.30pm; Sun: 8.30am-10pm
Bakery, Mon-Sat: 8am-12midnight; Sun: 8.30am-10pm

THE QUALITY CHOP HOUSE & SHOP

Beautifully preserved 150-year-old eating-house that's been sympathetically updated and expanded. There are two rooms, one retains its original layout and hard wooden booths, the other is newer and more comfortable but still redolent of an earlier era. The food is uncompromising: excellent produce, simply done. Adjoining the restaurant is a butcher and grocer. Be sure to try the housemade meat pies.

88-94 Farringdon Road, EC1R 3EA
Tel: 020 7278 1452
Mon-Sat: 12noon-3pm & 6am-11pm; Sun: 12noon-4pm

RANDALL & AUBIN

The wooden fittings and marble counters of this old butcher's shop give a casual atmosphere, with diners perched on stools as they tuck into plates of fish, seafood and frites, washed down with champagne. It's informal but glamorous, a touch of Old Soho that's as enjoyable on a hot summer's day as a rain-soaked winter night.

14-16 Brewer Street, W1F 0SG
Tel: 020 7287 4447
Mon-Thu: 12noon-11pm; Fri-Sat: 12noon-12midnight;
Sun: 12noon-10pm

REGENCY CAFÉ

The unspoiled 1940s moderne exterior has seen frequent use in photo shoots, TV shows and films looking for an authentic backdrop. In fact looks alone would be enough to recommend the Regency, but come here too for an exemplary fry-up. A note on etiquette: before taking a seat, place orders at the counter. Only then do you find a seat and listen out for your order, 'cheese omelette and chips twice!'

17-19 Regency Street, SW1P 4BY
Tel: 020 7821 6596
Mon-Fri: 7am-2.30pm & 6pm-7.15pm; Sat: 7am-12noon

ROCHELLE CANTEEN

In what was a school, once an integral part of the surrounding Boundary Estate (London's first social housing), are now artists' studios and this charming restaurant, serving simple and excellent British food (Barnsley chop and swede mash; chicken, leek and bacon pie). The atmosphere is relaxed, with communal dining at long tables, refectory-style. On sunny days, the lawn is a particularly inviting place to digest. Note: unlicensed, corkage is £6.50 per bottle.

Rochelle School, Arnold Circus, E2 7ES
Tel: 020 7729 5677
Sun-Wed: 9am-4.30pm; Thu-Sat: 9am-4.30pm & 6pm-10pm

ROTI KING

Outstanding Malaysian food – fluffy, buttery roti; dark, intensely aromatic curry and dhal; rich, eggy noodles – at bargain basement prices. The latter perhaps because the restaurant is actually in a basement, at the bottom of rather grimy steps on a sidestreet by Euston Station. None of which matters, the food is quite wonderful and queues stretching down the street are well deserved. Note: cash only, BYO allowed with £10 corkage per table.

Ian Hamilton House, Doric Way, NW1 1LH
Tel: 020 7387 2518
Mon-Sat: 12noon-3pm & *5pm-10.30pm*

ROTORINO

Bare brick and glamorous 1970s-style tiles sum up the casual yet refined approach of this popular Dalston restaurant, set up by chef wunderkind Stevie Parle. The cooking is Southern Italian-influenced, using the freshest British ingredients to deliver dishes that are subtle yet robust. Extra points for booths, a separate bar, and allowing reservations.

434 Kingsland Rd, E8 4AA
Tel: 020 7249 9081
Mon-Fri: 6pm-12midnight; Sat: 5pm-12midnight;
Sun: 12noon-12midnight

ROYAL CHINA

Opulent, old fashioned dining, particularly popular with large groups. Banquets aside, anyone can enjoy the very superior Cantonese cooking – dim sum is notably good – that keeps customers coming back, despite higher-than-average prices and service that can be curt.

24-26 Baker Street, W1U 3BZ
Tel: 020 7487 4688
Mon-Thu: 12noon- 11pm; Fri: 12noon-11.30pm; Sat: 12noon-11.30pm; Sun: 11am-10pm

RULES / UPSTAIRS AT RULES

For anyone who aspires to membership of a London gentleman's club, a couple of drinks here may come a close second. Situated above the capital's oldest surviving restaurant (opened 1798), Upstairs At Rules is supremely comfortable, with paneled walls, plush seating, no music to disrupt the burble of conversation, and the hubbub of Covent Garden obscured through leaded windows. All of which is recommendation enough, a cocktail menu that is the very definition of small but perfectly formed confirms its appeal.

35 Maiden Lane, WC2E 7LB
Tel: 020 7836 5314
Daily: 12noon-12midnight

SCOOTERCAFFE

There's little room for individuality in London's cafés, so enjoy this exception. A slightly rough around the edges enterprise, with tattered old posters on the walls and foraged furniture, it has a relaxed, bohemian air. During the day, enjoy coffee and cake, as evening approaches ties are loosened and hair let down with negronis, spritz, wine and beer.

132 Lower Marsh, SE1 7AE
Tel: 020 7620 1421
Mon-Thu: 8.30am-11pm; Fri: 8.30am-12midnight;
Sat: 10am-12midnight; Sun: 12noon-10pm

SCOTTI'S SNACK BAR

After loading up on reading material at nearby magCulture (p110), settle down in one of the city's few surviving classic 20th century cafés. The friendly proprietors serve proper tea and good sandwiches in a peaceful environment little changed in 50-odd years: plain wooden chairs and tables, patterned grey Formica wall panels and for decoration, a selection of small paintings and pot plants.

38 Clerkenwell Green, EC1R 0DU
Tel: 020 7253 8676
Mon-Fri: 8am-5pm

THE SEVEN STARS

Its proximity to the Royal Courts of Justice
makes this ancient pub a favourite with judges,
lawyers and journalists looking for refreshment.
Cat-lovers like it too – there's a long-standing
tradition that the resident feline wears an
Elizabethan ruff. Watch out for what may be
London's steepest staircase.

53-54 Carey Street, WC2A 2JB
Tel: 020 7242 8521
Mon-Fri: 11am-11pm; Sat: 12noon-11pm;
Sun: 12noon-10.30pm

SICHUAN-FOLK

Cantonese cooking dominates London's
Chinese restaurants, so it's always a pleasure
to find a little diversity. One sterling example
is this modest place, just off Brick Lane, which
has a kitchen specialising in lip-blisteringly hot
Szechuan food. Substantial weekday lunch deals
are a spectacular bargain at £7; pork belly with
buns, and green beans with shredded pork are
both recommended.

32 Hanbury Street, E1 6QR
Tel: 020 7247 4735
Mon-Fri: 12noon-10.30pm; Sat: 12.30pm-11pm;
Sun: 12.30pm-10.30pm

ST. JOHN BREAD & WINE

Yes, their wonderful bread and wine is for sale – but there's a restaurant, too, with separate menus for breakfast, lunch and supper, all of which feature excellent ingredients inventively prepared. You are likely to encounter kippers, mutton, piccalilli, oysters, seaweed and tongue, though happily not all on the same plate.

94-96 Commercial Street, E1 6LZ
Tel: 020 7251 0848
Mon: 8am-4pm & 6pm-10pm;
Tue-Fri: 8am-4pm & 6pm-11pm;
Sat: 8.30am-12noon & 1pm-4pm & 6pm-11pm;
Sun: 8.30am-12noon & 1pm-4pm & 6pm-10pm
Bar, Sun-Mon: 12noon-10pm; Tue-Sat: 12noon-11pm

ST. JOHN MALTBY

As with all Fergus Henderson's eateries, on offer is a disconcerting mixture of comfort food and Hammer Horror: bloodcake, blood oranges, Devilled kidneys; posset, prunes and asparagus. But anchovy toast and tea is a snack that warrants all the acclaim directed at St. John, and this utilitarian railway arch is a good spot to watch the market's bustle.

41 Maltby Street, SE1 3PA
Tel: 020 7553 9844
Wed-Thu: 5pm-10pm; Fri: 12noon-3.30pm & 5.30pm-10pm;
Sat: 10am-10pm; Sun: 10am-4pm

SUSHINOEN

In an unlovely stretch of Whitechapel near Aldgate East, it's a treat to find this warm and welcoming Japanese restaurant which has a broad menu that includes many homestyle dishes. Lunches are very good value, but not alarmingly so – after all, no one should be eating cheap sushi. Evening meals can be a little more elaborate, although still informal and unpretentious.

2 White Church Lane, E1 7QR
Tel: 020 3645 6734
Mon-Fri: 12noon-2.30pm & 6pm-10.30pm;
Sat: 12noon-10.30pm; Sun: 12noon-10pm

SWEETINGS

A resolutely old-fashioned City Boy spot, its appeal is as much for atmosphere as food, although fish and seafood is always fresh and well prepared. A seat at the counter is the way to go, and frequently the only option, such is its popularity. White sliced bread pre-spread with lots of butter, lashings of champagne, Chablis and oysters. How anyone gets any work done after lunch here, we have no idea.

39 Queen Victoria Street, EC4N 4SF
Tel: 020 7248 3062
Mon-Fri: 11.30am-3pm

Other branches
➦ 193 Balham
High Road,
SW12 9BE
➦ 44A Cannon
Street, EC4N 6JJ

TARO

Simple, inexpensive and unpretentious Japanese food that's best enjoyed at one of the counter seats, perched on the edge of the open kitchen. Taro opened in 1999, long before London was gripped by ramen mania; recent openings may be a hotter ticket but this remains a reliable and relaxed standby. If it's busy, choose from one of the many other Japanese restaurants at this end of Brewer Street.

61 Brewer Street, W1F 9UW
Tel: 020 7734 5826
Mon-Thu: 12noon-10.30pm;
Fri-Sat: 12noon-11pm; Sun: 12.30pm-9.30pm

TAQUERIA

Soft corn and flour tortillas are made in-house and used to great effect topped with or rolled around tasty meats and vegetables as quesadillas, tacos and tostadas. Small groups are best served here, allowing plenty of opportunity for tasting and sharing, although an order of tacos at the counter would be nice meal for one. Micheladas, a rare treat in this city, are recommended; a choice of beers and cocktails is available too, along with authentic aguas frescas.

141-145 Westbourne Grove, W11 2RS
Tel: 020 7229 4734
Mon-Thu: 12noon-11pm;
Fri-Sat: 12noon-11.30pm;
Sun: 12noon-10.30pm

TAYYABS

Such is Tayyabs' popularity that they've expanded into several adjacent shops and even underground, but still the queues keep growing. The menu is unchanging, offering simple Pakistani-Punjabi food of the very highest quality – grilled lamb chops, dahl with baby aubergine and bitter gourd are all standouts. The enormous turnover keeps prices low, but at busy times (from about 6.30pm any day of the week) it can feel almost dementedly frantic.

83-89 Fieldgate Street, E1 1JU
Tel: 020 7247 6400
Daily: 12noon-11pm

Also worth waiting for
➻ Bao Bar, p11
➻ Barbary, p13
➻ Honey & Co, p36
➻ Padella, p49

THE THREE KINGS

An amiable, eccentric pub that caters to a truly mixed group of patrons, many of whom have been regulars since a time when the vinyl jukebox wasn't a novelty. Gin is a particular speciality here, but imbibers of every stripe will find plenty to appeal. It is cheerfully ramshackle, with outlandish décor (the rhino head is unmissable), quiz nights and a contagious air of bonhomie.

7 Clerkenwell Close, EC1R 0DY
Tel: 020 7253 0483
Mon-Fri: 12noon-11pm; Sat: 5.30pm-11pm

YAUATCHA

Chinese food of a particularly sophisticated type: tea shop, patisserie and restaurant, with the focus on dim sum, presenting food that's as pretty as it is delicious. The dramatically-lit downstairs restaurant is a pleasant escape on a dark, rainy lunchtime or at night, but for brighter days, the ground floor may be preferable. Patisserie and tea, also at street level, make for a

Just a few doors away
➺ Yauatcha owner Alan Yau's Duck And Rice (90 Berwick Street, W1F 0QB), another modern riff on traditional Chinese cooking. It's a little more casual, but still unerringly chic.

glamorous pit stop. Exquisite baked goods are also available to take away, wrapped and packaged to make a wonderful gift.

15-17 Broadwick Street, W1F 0DL
Tel: 020 7494 8888
Sun-Thu: 12noon-10pm; Fri-Sat: 12noon-10.30pm
Patisserie, daily: 12noon-11pm

FOOD SHOPS

ALGERIAN COFFEE STORES

Since 1887 this has been a place to buy the ingredients and equipment essential to the preparation of coffee and tea. Beans are available in dozens of varieties – huge sacks of them are piled behind the counter – they're sold by weight, whole or ground to the customer's requirements. There's tea too – India, China, Ceylon, fruit, herbal, matcha – available loose or packaged. Also a range of Italian and Turkish stovetops, French cafetieres, Vietnamese filters and classic cones, along with grinders, tea pots, strainers and caddies, spare parts and even stainless steel trivets for gas cookers. And for those on the move, they serve excellent espresso to take away for the bargain price of £1.

52 Old Compton Street, W1V 6PB
Tel: 020 7437 2480
Mon-Wed: 9am-7pm; Thu & Fri: 9am-9pm; Sat: 9am-8pm

ANDROUET

The slick London outpost of a centenarian French cheesemonger, Androuet has a rather smart persona but a distinctly friendly welcome. Rather than showcase only Gallic cheese, they concentrate on a selection of seasonal Continental and British fare, with

100 or so varieties available at any time, around 20 of which are dependent on time of year – one of the best is the highly original Mayfield, an English take on Emmenthal, produced in East Sussex.

Old Spitalfields Market, Commercial Street, E1 6BG
Tel: 020 7375 3168
Shop, Mon-Sun: 10am-7pm
Restaurant, Wed: 5pm-10.30pm;
Thu-Sat: 12noon-10.30pm; Sun: 12noon-9pm

BRICK LANE BEIGEL BAKE

Of course the beigels are the draw at this stalwart bakery and all-night eatery, but the loaves of black rye (available at weekends only) also deserve a mention, as does the tea: strong, stewed and served in polystyrene cups, it is magnificently invigorating. Eating in is an option, although only at the shallow counter. To pick up a dozen bagels for the week ahead and chew on a filled one amid the gathered throng in the early hours of Sunday morning has long been a London rite of passage.

159 Brick Lane, E1 6SB
Tel: 020 7729 0616
Daily: 24 hours

CUNDALL & GARCIA

An independent holdout amid the chain franchises of Spitalfields market. A green awning and wooden bench entices visitors to this artfully old-fashioned deli, housed in a Grade II listed building. It's the village shop reimagined, with jars of striped candy canes in the window, rows of classic penny sweets and pretty little tins of tea and fudge. Lunchtimes are deservedly busy, with sandwiches (chicken schnitzel; roast turkey, chilli jam), Scotch eggs and hot food to take away.

42 Brushfield Street, E1 6AG
Tel: 020 7247 2487
Mon-Fri: 10am-4pm; Sat: 12noon-5pm

GAZZANOS

This little corner of Clerkenwell was once known as Little Italy for its concentration of Italian immigrants. Over the 20th century, most dispersed but Gazzanos, the nearby St Peter's church and a few other holdouts survive. Now well over 100 years in business, the store remains in the tender care of the original family. A few years ago it was forced to remodel (in fact the entire building was demolished and rebuilt), but despite superficial changes it has the whiff of authenticity: a

tantalising blend of cured meat and cheese is
the defining aroma, and there's the mandatory
selection of dried pastas. While the city
constantly drifts and shifts, the family Gazzano
keep a firm grip on this very special place.

167-169 Farringdon Road, EC1R 3AL
Tel: 020 7837 1586
Tue-Fri: 8.30am-5.30pm;
Sat: 9am-5.30pm; Sun: 10am-2pm

GERRY'S WINES & SPIRITS

The first and last port of call for anyone on
the hunt for out-of-the-ordinary booze. There
are dozens of varieties of rum, vodka, gin and
whisky, as well as vermouth, aperitifs, digestifs,
liqueurs and bitters. There are also novelties:
six-litre bottles of vodka, Day of the Dead-
themed tequilas and porn star Ron Jeremy's
own brand of rum. To guide you through all this
are expert staff, with free tastings to tempt you
into a reckless purchase.

74 Old Compton Street, W1D 4UW
Tel: 020 7734 2053 / 020 7734 4215
Mon-Thu: 9am-7.30pm; Fri-Sat: 9am-9pm;
Sun: 12noon-6pm

GOLDEN GATE BAKERY

Chinese buns and baked goods are the order of
the day: char siu buns, curry buns, sausage and
egg buns, almond buns, butter buns, pandan
sponge cakes, lotus seed balls and egg tarts. It's
a tight little space that has a sort of unofficial
one-way system; start on the left, finish at the
till. Grab tongs and a tray at the door and work
your way from savoury to sweet. If the trays
are empty, fresh supplies usually arrive in a few
minutes.

13 Macclesfield Street, W1D 5PR
Tel: 020 7287 9862
Daily: 10.30am-9pm

I CAMISA

Join an orderly queue and wait for an assistant
at the counter to take your order for meats,
cheese, tomatoes, rocket, basil, canned and
bottled goods or wonderful homemade pasta.
This venerable family-run Italian deli has
lost none of its old world charm, with wood
and glass drawers and terrazzo floor and an
atmosphere that marks it out as among the last
of the breed.

61 Old Compton Street, W1D 6HS
Tel: 020 7437 7610
Mon-Sat: 8.30am-6pm

LINA STORES

The prettiest of London's historic Italian delicatessens, its signature mint-green awning stands out on this garish Soho strip. Fresh pasta has been made on site for the past 70 years. Each day you'll find an array of up to 10 different tortellini, ravioli, mezzalunas, from pumpkin and amaretti, through to smoked mozzarella and aubergine dusted in semolina in trays behind the counter. An A-Z of Italian cheeses, cured meats (don't miss the wild-boar salami), and library of every dried-pasta shape imaginable, enticingly displayed, make this a feast for the eyes as much as it is for the stomach.

8 Brewer Street, W1F 0SH
Tel: 020 7437 6482
Mon-Tue: 8.30am-7.30pm;
Wed-Fri: 8.30am-8.30pm;
Sat: 10am-7.30pm; Sun: 11am-5pm

For a taste of Old Soho
➻ Algerian Coffee Stores, p66
➻ Bar Italia, p12
➻ I Camisa, p70
➻ New Evaristo Club, p48

LOON FUNG SUPERMARKET

As its motto goes, Loon Fung is 'for the Chinese in you'. Every food group is covered here: aisles of vegetables (it's good for picking up daikon, durian, star fruit, bitter melon, snake beans), pantry ingredients (rice, noodles, flours and condiments) through to the pungent butcher counter at the back bearing stacks of pig trotters, ears and slabs of belly. Anyone attempting to explore their Chinese side in this hectic and unabashedly authentic store should brace themselves for an extreme shopping mission, one that may involve sharp-elbowed Chinese grandmothers.

42-44 Gerrard Street, W1D 5QG
Tel: 020 7437 7332
Daily: 10am-8pm

LO'S NOODLE FACTORY

Where Chinatown's main drag, Gerrard Street, seems primarily a honeypot for tourists, this alleyway that runs parallel is another world entirely. Narrow and unadorned, it's home to a fish and seafood stall, a vegetable shop and this factory, which is really little more than a room. There's no browsing, orders are taken as you stand in the hallway, just ask for what you want from a choice of rice noodle rolls (cheung fun), flat rice noodles (ho fun) or buns, all fresh, ready for steaming or frying and remarkably inexpensive.

6 Dansey Place, W1D 6EZ
Mon-Sun: 6am-6.30pm

MARKUS COFFEE

In 1957, long before Londoners walked the streets with coffee cups permanently attached, Mr and Mrs Markus set up shop in a quiet Bayswater street, roasting and blending coffee for the cognoscenti. The business has since passed to a former employee who maintains the same quality, selling 34 varieties of bean from 13 different countries. And if none of their blends is right for your palate, you can even make your own. The shop has much of its original charm, with the roaster in the window, bags of beans along the counter and neat, steel cases of blends behind it. Room has been made for a few tables, ideal for a pick-me-up en route to or from nearby Hyde Park.

13 Connaught Street, W2 2AY
Tel: 020 7723 4020 / 020 7262 4630
Mon-Sat: 8.30am-5.30pm

For your shopping list
New Loon Moon is one of the few London shops to sell Moon cakes, only available during the Autumn festival

NEW LOON MOON

Gerrard Street, the beating heart of London's Chinatown, is ever the cultural eye opener. Occupying the only surviving purpose-built 18th-century tavern building (look for the plaque outside), New Loon Moon crams every ingredient of the Southeast Asian gastronomic repertoire into its warren of interlinking rooms. This is a one-stop shop for sauces, oils, wonton wrappers, tofu, frozen fish, glutinous rice flours and a good range of Asian greens, including pea aubergines and petai.

9a Gerrard Street, W1D 5PN
Tel: 020 7734 3887
Mon-Sat: 10.30am-8pm

PAXTON & WHITFIELD

Sandwiched between elegant gentleman's tailors and shoe shops, gold on black lettering marks the spot of this historic cheesemonger dating back to 1797. The counter choice is impressive, especially the vast range of blues from England, Wales, Spain, France and Italy. But their own-branded range of biscuits (the charcoal and malted varieties are

a delight) and preserves (gooseberry chutney
and confit white fig among them) are mighty
vessels for these fine fromages. And we confess
a weakness too for their bright yellow tote bags.

93 Jermyn Street, SW1Y 6JE
Tel: 020 7930 0259
Mon-Sat: 10am-6.30pm; Sun: 11am-5pm

PHOENICIA MEDITERRANEAN FOOD HALL

Mediterranean Food Hall seems a suitably
vague description for a shop selling everything
from toilet tissue and baklava to Mexican
chillies and udon noodles. But this substantial
supermarket definitely does specialise in
Mediterranean produce, with its buckets
of glistening olives and pickled aubergines,
through to the floor-to-ceiling pasta wall and a
fridge devoted to every halloumi and feta brand
under the sun. Perhaps best of all is their meat
counter, filled with enticing cuts and a range
of marinated lamb, chicken and fish, which are
ideal if you're pressed for time.

186-192 Kentish Town Road, NW5 2AE
Tel: 020 7267 1267
Mon-Sat: 9am-8pm; Sun: 10am-6pm

RICE WINE SHOP

As the name suggests, this tiny grocery shop is good for picking up sake, but it's not limited to that. Come here too for a selection of Japanese ingredients which, while not exhaustive, is reliable. They have very good fresh sushi to take away every day, which is ideal if you feel like an inexpensive snack sitting outside in nearby Golden Square.

82 Brewer Street, W1F 9UA
Tel: 020 7439 3705
Mon-Fri: 10am-9pm; Sun: 12noon-8pm

TAJ STORES

Yellow neon lettering loudly and proudly spells out the name of this Brick Lane establishment specialising in Asian foodstuffs. A family-run business in operation since 1938, it services the local Bangladeshi community and restaurants. Set aside some time to explore this spacious store, a proper rummage uncovers all manner of spices, sacks of rice large enough to see you through a decade of curries, a greengrocer, halal butcher and even a section devoted to massive stockpots in which to cook it all.

112 Brick Lane, E1 6RL
Tel: 020 7377 0061
Daily: 9am-9pm

TURKISH FOOD CENTRE

Evidence gathered here suggests that while many of us might struggle to get through a single box of dried parsley in our lives, others are buying it by the kilo. Bulk-buying, though clearly an option, is certainly not mandatory. There's a grand pick of produce all year round, a butcher's counter, Turkish pastries piled in pyramids, even a section of barbeque equipment. Not a penny is wasted on merchandising and low prices will have you double-checking you haven't been undercharged.

89 Ridley Road, E8 2NH
Tel: 020 7254 6754
Daily: 24 hours

Other branches
➥ 363 Fore Street, N9 0NR
➥ 542-544 Lordship Lane, N22 5BY
➥ 88 Green Lanes, N13 5UP
➥ 2-8 Winchester Road, E4 9LN

SHOPS

A PORTUGUESE LOVE AFFAIR

A panoply of products from Portugal for every aspect of the home. There are beautifully packaged Claus Porto soaps, blankets, ceramics, old-fashioned toys, stationery, cards and varieties of tinned fish including octopus in olive oil, spiced calamari, roes of hake and smoked sardines. Not everyday essentials then, but excellent for gifts.

142 Columbia Road, E2 7RG
Tel: 020 7613 1482
Wed-Thu: 12noon-7pm; Fri: 12noon-6pm;
Sat: 11am-6pm; Sun: 9.30am-5pm

AIME

Parisian-style women's clothing and accessories, with a sprinkling of homewares. Understated and chic, expect plenty of Isabel Marant and Sessun along with Repetto pumps (they were among the first British stockists). Next door is APC, with whom they share a similar, though in that case unisex, aesthetic. There's also a second, larger West London branch of Aimé (32 Ledbury Road, W11 2AB; Tel: 020 7221 7070).

17 Redchurch Street, E2 7DJ
Tel: 020 7739 2158
Mon-Fri: 11am-7pm; Sat: 10am-7pm; Sun: 12noon-5pm

ALFIES ANTIQUE MARKET

Long established home to dozens of dealers, their items running the gamut from large pieces of furniture to jewellery, most of it from the last century, with pieces ranging from a few pounds to several thousand. Housed in an Art Deco department store building, it's a winning mix of shabby and glamorous with a rooftop restaurant that's a hidden delight. Church Street is home to many furniture and clothing dealers, as well as a lively traditional street market.

13-25 Church Street, NW8 8DT
Tel: 020 7723 6066
Tue-Sat: 10am-6pm

ARTHUR BEALE

Much is made of the incongruity of a ship's chandler in Covent Garden, and it's true that at first glance it's an unlikely location to find such a wide selection of porthole covers and rigging. Closer examination reveals plenty of items as suited to the city as they are the high seas: whistles, floating cork key rings, duct tape in an array of colours and Saint James striped T-shirts.

194 Shaftesbury Avenue, WC2H 8JP
Tel: 020 7836 9034
Mon-Wed: 10am-7pm; Thu: 10am-8pm;
Fri-Sat: 10am-7pm; Sun: 11am-5pm

B SOUTHGATE

Ben Southgate is a finder and supplier of superior vintage furniture and objets, much of which is utilitarian in style: shop displays, sturdy storage, café chairs, packing crates, toys, clocks and lights all feature. Some items are sensitively restored but none suffers the ignominy of 'upcycling'.

4 The Courtyard, Ezra Street, E2 7RH
Tel: 079 0596 0792
Sun: 9am-4pm

B1866

The first shop to be opened by Brooks, 150-year-old makers of bicycle saddles, clothing and accessories. It looks like a contemporary menswear shop with its painted brick walls and colourful displays of covetable items, including the company's saddles available in custom colours from their Birmingham factory, bags using a 1950s design, and a range of small leather goods, baskets, rain ponchos and helmets.

36 Earlham Street, WC2H 9LH
Tel: 020 7836 9968
Mon-Sat: 11am-7pm; Sun: 12noon-6pm

BLADE RUBBER STAMPS

Anyone who pays bills, or requests their payment, knows the satisfaction of marking an invoice with PAID in red ink. Blade offer simple stamps such as this, as well as more ornate ones for decorative purposes. Best of all, they operate a fast, efficient and inexpensive service for personalised designs.

12 Bury Place, WC1A 2JL
Tel: 020 7831 4123
Mon-Sat: 10.30am-6pm; Sun: 11.30am-4.30pm

BOROUGH KITCHEN

From the humble cookie cutter up, this shop has everything for the well-appointed kitchen. Selections are made with quality in mind, so even a potato peeler can command a hefty price (£18 for the Kai Select), but if it's the best you require, this is where to come. Cooking classes at all levels are available, from Knife Skills to Steak Knowledge.

Other branches
➻ 1B-1C Hampstead High Street, NW3 1RG
➻ 86 Chiswick High Road, W4 1PP

16 Borough High Street, SE1 9QG
Tel: 020 3302 4260
Mon-Fri: 10am-7pm; Sat: 9am-6pm; Sun: 11am-5pm

CHESS AND BRIDGE

You needn't be a grand master to appreciate this highly specialist shop; beginners are as welcome as experts, and the selection extends well beyond the titular, including backgammon, poker, Scrabble and a wide selection of board games. On fine days, boards are set up outside for anyone to use.

44 Baker Street, W1U 7RT
Tel: 020 7486 7015 / 020 7288 1305
Mon-Wed: 9.30am-6pm; Thu: 9.30am-7pm;
Fri-Sat: 9.30am-6pm; Sun: 11am-5pm

CHOOSING KEEPING

Stationery doesn't excite everyone, but its devotees are ardent and will find much to admire in this little shop, precision-packed with items for writing, drawing and organising. Japanese and German products feature heavily, along with intriguing deadstock vintage items. Come here for rollerballs, pencils, felt tips and erasers; staplers, scissors, notepaper and desk tidies, not forgetting own-label wallets and coin purses.

128 Columbia Road, E2 7RG
Tel: 020 7613 3842
Wed-Sat: 11.30am-7pm; Sun: 9.30am-5pm

CLAIRE DE ROUEN BOOKS

A narrow, scruffy staircase is the unprepossessing entrance to what David Bailey once called 'maybe the best photography bookshop in the world'. The limited space is well used, crammed with photography titles as well as art, architecture and design, from publishers around the world.

First Floor, 125 Charing Cross Road, WC2H 0EW
Tel: 020 7287 1813
Tue-Sat: 12noon-7pm

THE CLOTH HOUSE

Dressmaking fabrics sourced from all over the world: printed cottons, shirting, needlecord, drill, wool, jersey, linen, silk and denim, along with a wide variety of buttons, ribbons and trim, many of which are are vintage. It's not cheap, but the buying is excellent and staff are knowledgeable.

47 Berwick Street, W1F 8SJ
Tel: 020 7437 5155
Mon-Fri: 9.30am-6pm; Sat: 10.30am-6pm

Three more for the dressmaker
➥ Crescent Trading, p87
➥ Liberty, p109
➥ Ray Stitch, p113

COMPTON NEWS

Stop in here for Italian Vogue, French Marie Claire, US Esquire, Die Zeit, Le Monde and dozens of small press titles.

48 Old Compton Street, W1D 4UA
Tel: 020 7437 2479
Mon-Sat: 6am-10pm; Sun: 10am-10pm

CONSERVATORY ARCHIVES

The phrase urban jungle takes on an entirely different meaning in the two rooms of this shop, each completely packed with plants, some of which trail from the ceiling, others rising up from pots to meet them. Succulents, ferns and cacti dominate, vying for light with Monsteras and hanging Strings Of Pearls.

493-495 Hackney Road, E2 9ED
Tel: 07785 522 762
Tue-Fri: 12noon-7pm; Sat-Sun: 11.30am-7pm

COUVERTURE & THE GARBSTORE

Clothing for men, women, children along with a wide range of home furnishings and stationery, all arranged in perfect Instagram-ready colour-coordinated displays. Prices range from low to high – there are Japanese mugs for just £9 and dresses in excess of £500 – with an emphasis on collaborations and labels that are hard to find

in the UK (Mina Perhonen, Hansel from Basel,
Raquel Allegra, Apiece Apart).

188 Kensington Park Road, W11 2ES
Tel: 020 7229 2178
Mon-Sat: 10am-6pm; Sun: 12noon-5pm

CRESCENT TRADING

A warehouse-like shop, known for good quality
fabric (silks, cotton poplin, wool) from reputable
sources. It's popular with trade customers,
which is an indication of the keen pricing, but
amateurs are welcome too.

Unit 2, Quaker Court, 41 Quaker Street, E1 6SN
Tel: 020 7377 5067
Mon-Thu: 9.30am-5pm; Fri: 9.30am-2pm; Sun: 9am-2pm

D R HARRIS

There's nothing to stop you buying a packet
of painkillers at this centuries-old chemist,
but their own products are what set it apart.
Cologne, soap and skincare products come in
scents of lavender, almond, sandalwood and
their own blends. Along with an excellent range
of clippers, scissors, brushes and shoehorns, it's a
favourite place for gifts – or to cheer yourself up.

29 St James's Street, SW1A 1HB
Tel: 020 7930 3915
Mon-Fri: 8.30am-6pm; Sat: 9.30am-5pm

DAUNT BOOKS

Other branches
➟ 61 Cheapside, EC2V 6AX
➟ 158-164 Fulham Road, SW10 9PR
➟ 112-114 Holland Park Avenue, W11 4UA
➟ 51 South End Road, NW3 2QB
➟ 193 Haverstock Hill, NW3 4QL

Arguably London's most beautiful bookshop with an original Edwardian interior and long book-lined galleries. It's one of the very best too, with knowledgeable and helpful staff who demonstrate an unerring knack for displaying the wares.

83 Marylebone High Street, W1U 4QW
Tel: 020 7224 2295
Mon-Sat: 9am-7.30pm; Sun: 11am-6pm

DOVER STREET MARKET

The move from Dover Street to Haymarket in 2016 brought greater floorspace, with the brands (Comme des Garçons, Loewe, Raf Simons, Fendi and Celine among them) gathered around a central staircase, giving the feel of a mixed artist group show. The sole British outpost of Anglo-French café The Rose Bakery on the top floor is well worth visiting.

18-22 Haymarket, SW1Y 4DG (entrance on Orange Street)
Tel: 020 7518 0680
Mon-Sat: 11am-7pm; Sun: 12noon-6pm

DRAKE'S FACTORY SHOP

Known for understated, well-cut British-made menswear bringing the merest hint of the contemporary to classic styles – all of which comes at a cost. At this shop however, it's possible to find pieces from past seasons at affordable prices. Scarves, ties and knitwear are often well represented, look out too for shirts, trousers and accessories.

3 Haberdasher Street, N1 6ED
Tel: 020 7993 0899
Mon-Fri: 10am-5pm

EGG

Housed in a former dairy, hidden in a small Knightsbridge mews, egg is a womenswear boutique that stocks brands including Casey Casey, Sofie d'Hoore and dosa, as well as their own line which has an emphasis on an oversized and loose silhouette. The shop's visual displays are closer to art installations than mere window-dressing, so even if you don't buy anything (and be warned, prices are high), it's pleasure enough to browse.

36 Kinnerton Street, SW1X 8ES
Tel: 020 7235 9315
Mon-Sat: 10am-6pm

FARLOWS

In a substantial building once occupied by a bank, is everything devotees of huntin', shootin' and fishin' might desire. Even for a city-dweller it's not hard to envisage uses for Farlows' products. Hip flasks and hand warmers serve their purpose on moors, we're sure, but they are equally well-suited to windswept bus stops, and an Opinel knife would do as well for a piece of cheese on a picnic as it does gutting a small animal. The showstopper here is the fishing section, where anglers can buy the constituent parts to construct artificial flies of their own design. Whether you're a country gent or mere townie fantasist, this is the place.

9 Pall Mall, SW1Y 5NP
Tel: 020 7484 1000
Mon-Wed: 9am-6pm; Thu: 9am-7pm; Fri: 9am-6pm;
Sat: 10am-6pm; Sun: 11am-5pm

FORTNUM & MASON

It may be preposterous and puffed-up with its frock-coated staff and ornate decoration, but it's still quite irresistible. It was at the centre of the Georgian trade boom, offering since the 1700s a tremendous array of exotic spices, teas and meats and it retains much of its traditional charm. Of the shop's five restaurants, The St

James's is renowned for its tea, but we prefer The Fountain on the ground floor, which is a little less formal. Their Welsh Rarebit is delicious, suitably traditional and almost affordable.

181 Piccadilly, W1A 1ER
Tel: 020 7734 8040
Mon-Sat: 10am-8pm; Sun: 11.30am-6pm

FOYLES

One of the best known and best loved names in bookselling is flourishing in its second century. Founded in 1903, Foyles flagship store is in lavish new premises, a bold yet sympathetic reworking of the old Central St Martin's art school building. The space is light and airy, with intimate nooks for browsing and rummaging. Their stock, on four miles of shelves, is both broad and deep, with all genres and multiple languages catered. Dip into your purchases in the top floor café.

Other branches
➻ Southbank Centre, Riverside, SE1 8XX
➻ 74-75 Lower Ground Floor, Westfield Stratford City, E20 1EH
➻ Unit 22, Lower Concourse, Waterloo Station, SE1 8SW

107 Charing Cross Road, WC2H 0DT
Tel: 020 7437 5660
Mon-Sat: 9.30am-9pm; Sun: 11.30am-6pm

More favourite specialist shops
➤➤ Arthur Beale, p81
➤➤ Blade Rubber Stamps, p83
➤➤ Farlows, p90
➤➤ James Smith & Sons, p93
➤➤ Shepherds, p115

GARDNER'S MARKET SUNDRIESMEN

Everyone should find a reason to patronise this wonderful shop; a fourth-generation family business. The limited space is tightly packed with paper and polythene bags, canvas totes, balls of twine, stickers, price tags and other essentials for home, shop, market stall and office.

149 Commercial Street, E1 6BJ
Tel: 020 7247 5119
Mon-Fri: 6.30am-2.30pm

GOODHOOD STORE

At ground level are clothes for men and women, with a leaning towards casual items such as trainers, jogging pants and sweatshirts. Continue to the basement for an excellent selection of homewares and beauty products that's drawn from far and wide. With items ranging from small and affordable up to grand gestures, this is a regular port of call when a gift is needed.

151 Curtain Road, EC2A 3QE
Tel: 020 7729 3600
Mon-Fri 10.30am-6.30pm; Sat: 10.30am-7pm;
Sun: 12noon-6pm

GOSH!

Comics, graphic novels, manga, small press publications, coffee table retrospectives and original artwork are all present in this bright and spacious shop, arranged over two levels. It's also host to regular events, signings and launches, and they'll set up a standing order for your favourite reads too, holding titles as they come into stock for you to pick up at your convenience.

1 Berwick Street, W1F 0DR
Tel: 020 7636 1011
Daily: 10.30am-7pm

JAMES SMITH & SONS

It says much about London's climate that one of the few fully functioning relics of Victorian retail is an umbrella shop. James Smith's singular selection runs from the classic malacca-handled gent's brolly to the latest miniscule retractable, with choice so varied and desirable you may come to hope for rainy days. Their range of walking sticks is every bit as impressive including one model, complete with two glasses and a flask, based on one owned by Toulouse Lautrec.

53 New Oxford Street, WC1A 1BL
Tel: 020 7836 4731
Mon-Fri: 10am-5.45pm; Sat: 10am-5.15pm

JAPAN CENTRE

If a trip to Japan is out of the question, consider this the next best thing. Selling Japanese food and products in various West End locations since the 1970s, it was only in September 2017 that the Japan Centre opened this, its flagshop store. The focus is on the food hall, with large sections devoted to sake, tea and miso, as well as fresh produce (fish, meat, vegetables) and baked goods. For those unwilling or unable to cook, there's a dining area; look out too for tastings and cooking demos. But it's more than food, with an excellent selection of books and magazines as well as ceramics and tableware.

35b Panton Street, SW1Y 4EA
Tel: 020 3405 1246
Mon-Sat: 10am-9.30pm; Sun: 11am-8pm

Other branches
➥ Ceramic Store, 19 Shaftesbury Avenue, W1D 7ED
➥ Great Eastern Market, Westfield Stratford City, E20 1GL

JAPANESE KNIFE COMPANY

To categorise the Japanese Knife Company as mere sharpeners of knives does them a disservice, in truth the shop is more of a temple to the Japanese way with steel. But sharpen

Other branches
➥ 1C Kensington Church Walk, W8 4NB
➥ 8 Greek Street, W1D 4DG

knives they do, and at a reassuringly imperial 75p per inch. Of course, such is their enthusiasm that you may walk in with a Wüsthof and leave with something else entirely.

36 Baker Street, W1U 3EU
Tel: 020 7487 4868
Daily: 10.30am-6pm

JASPER MORRISON SHOP

While travelling the world pursuing his day job as one of the UK's most revered industrial designers and thinkers, Morrison assembles stock for this little shop that adjoins his design studio. Items are chosen for a combination of simple, understated design and utility, with an emphasis on tools and implements for the kitchen, office, workshop and garden.

Access is through a black door, next to a takeaway, visitors must buzz for entry.
24b Kingsland Road, E2 8DA
No phone
Mon-Fri: 11am-5pm (closed during August)

Great for gifts
➤ Couverture &
The Garbstore,
p86
➤ Goodhood
Store, p92
➤ Labour And
Wait, p98
➤ Luna &
Curious, p111
➤ Magma, p103
➤ Nook, p102
➤ Pentreath &
Hall, p111
➤ Present &
Correct, p112

JOHN BELL AND CROYDEN

The spacious, light premises are almost too chic for anyone suffering sniffles, but this is very much a dispensing pharmacy carrying the full panoply of modern healthcare, from pills, ointments and tinctures to vitamins, supplements and teas. In addition, there are beauty and grooming products, mobility aids and on-site specialist clinics.

50-54 Wigmore Street, W1U 2AU
Tel: 020 7935 5555
Mon-Fri: 8.30am-7pm; Sat: 9.30am-7pm; Sun: 12noon-6pm

JOHN SANDOE BOOKS

Anyone seeking the DNA of a classic bookshop from which to cultivate their own might wish to chip loose a sliver of paint from this paragon of the type. Arranged across three little houses over three cramped floors, it is both intimate and rambling, with every conceivable space employed for the display and storage of books of every type, their quality being a shared characteristic.

10-12 Blacklands Terrace, SW3 2SR
Tel: 020 7589 9473
Mon-Sat: 9.30am-6.30pm; Sun: 11am-5pm

JOHN SIMONS

US and European Ivy League and related clothing is draped across mid-century furniture, paintings and sculptures. There are unstructured J Keydge jackets from France, Pendleton shirts from Oregon, Japanese socks and an expanding range of own-brand creations, notably madras shirts and US-made loafers. The eponymous Mr Simons has been selling this sort of clothing since the mid-1950s, in shops from Hackney to Richmond. Now, ably assisted by his son Paul, this may be his best yet.

46 Chiltern Street, W1U 7QR
Tel: 020 3490 2729
Tue-Sat: 11am-6pm; Sun: 12noon-5pm

JP BOOKS

Crammed into an intimate space is an unrivalled range of Japanese books and magazines, catering to a diverse range of interests, including fashion, crafts, pets, cooking, health, language and travel guides. The gift and stationery section usually yields something interesting and so you never miss out, they set up subscriptions too.

24-25 Denman Street, W1D 7HU
Tel: 020 7839 4839
Mon-Sat: 10.30am-8pm; Sun: 11am-6pm

Other branches
➻ Serpentine
Gallery,
Kensington
Gardens, W2 3XA
➻ Whitechapel
Art Gallery,
80-82
Whitechapel
High Street,
E1 7QX

KOENIG BOOKS

An art bookshop, piled high with bulky
volumes and esoteric periodicals,
all neatly displayed and presented.
The downstairs section is every bit as
orderly and it's well-stocked too, with
a central table and floor-to-ceiling
shelves lining the walls. Best of all,
there are bargains in the true sense
of the word – items you might want
at full price, rather than just too cheap
to resist.

80 Charing Cross Road, WC2H 0BF
Tel: 020 7240 8190
Mon-Fri: 11am-8pm; Sat: 10am-8pm

LABOUR AND WAIT

Specialists in household items of
a hardy if austere nature, such as
enamel pans, wooden brushes and oil
lamps. These sit alongside durable
clothing, including French workwear,
Saint James cotton tops and knitwear,
and selections from Norfolk-based
clothiers, Old Town.

85 Redchurch Street, E2 7DJ
Tel: 020 7729 6253
Tue-Fri: 11am-6.30pm; Sat-Sun: 11am-6pm

LES SENTEURS

The millions spent on advertising by global fragrance brands mean nothing to the expert staff here who work patiently with customers to find the perfect scent for themselves or to give as a gift. As one would expect, the nose does much of the work, but when buying for others, many factors are taken into account to establish the appropriate perfume – and as a safeguard, they'll always provide a tester too. The overpowering funk of department stores and duty free counters is a far cry from this calm, fragrant environment, home to specialist makers of perfumes, colognes, bath products and candles such as Frederic Malle, Creed, Bruno Acampora, Molinard and Robert Piguet.

71 Elizabeth Street, SW1W 9PJ
Tel: 020 7730 2322
Mon-Sat: 10am-6pm

Other branches
➻ 2 Seymour Place, W1H 7NA

LEVI'S VINTAGE CLOTHING STORE

This is a place to pick up reproduction 501s from the 1930s to 1970s, which are the backbone of the shop, supplemented by T-shirts, jackets and accessories from seasonal ranges that take inspiration from the company's archive.

5 Newburgh Street, W1F 7RB
Tel: 020 7287 4941
Mon-Wed: 11am-6.30pm; Thu: 11am-7pm;
Fri-Sat: 11am-6.30pm; Sun: 12noon-5pm

LEWIS LEATHERS

Home of the British biker jacket, the company's roots stretch back to the 1890s, their sturdy weatherproof leather gear outfitting early motorists and flyers, and even the RAF in World War Two, only finding its niche as makers of biker wear in the 1950s. Today, from premises off Tottenham Court Road, they sell many of their classic styles, with options for customisation and bespoke to a core clientele of bikers, rock stars and those who aspire to be one, the other, or both.

3-5 Whitfield Street, W1T 2SA
Tel: 020 7636 4314
Mon-Sat: 11am-6pm

LIBERTY

The city's loveliest department store, a mock-Tudor confection that uses salvaged wood from battleships for the wood-paneled interior. Luxury goods are the stock in trade: scarves (the scarf room is legendary); handbags; fragrance; boots and shoes; clothing for men and women; decorative items including rugs and antiques; and of course Liberty print fabrics.

Great Marlborough Street, W1B 5AH
Tel: 020 7734 1234
Mon-Sat: 10am-8pm; Sun: 12noon-6pm

LIBRERIA

With any book we want available online, bookshops are finding new ways to appeal to customers. This one does so with an approach that abandons traditional categories, encouraging discovery with themed sections: 'dark days', 'madonnas, mothers & whores', 'enlightenment'. All of which, along with little nooks in which to cosy up, careful lighting and a no phone policy, make it so suited for browsing that some might prefer it to their own home.

65 Hanbury Street, E1 5JP
Tel: 020 3818 3240
Tue-Wed: 10am-6pm; Thu-Sat: 11am-10pm;
Sun: 12noon-6pm

LUNA & CURIOUS

Less heralded than nearby Redchurch Street, Calvert Avenue has a healthy sprinkling of independent shops, that can be relied on for treats on dull days or when a thoughtful gift is needed. Here, smart buying mixes women's clothing with homewares, stationery and magazines, and always turns up something charming and unusual.

24-26 Calvert Avenue, E2 7JP
Tel: 020 3222 0034
Mon-Sat: 11am-6pm; Sun: 11am-5pm

MAGCULTURE

Magazine lovers worldwide follow Jeremy Leslie's magCulture website and accompanying events, without question the best source for news, interviews and debate about periodical publishing. Since late 2015, magCulture is a shop too, housed appropriately in an old newsagent, on the route from Clerkenwell to Angel. The vigorous good health of small press publishers is clear to see in the variety – and heft – of titles from across the globe, showed to great effect on timeless Vitsoe 606 shelving.

270 St John Street, EC1V 4PE
Tel:.020 3759 8022
Mon-Fri: 11am-7pm; Sat: 12noon-5pm

MAGMA

A broad, engaging mix of books, magazines, stationery, toys, bags, prints and products. Too arty to be a gift shop and too light-hearted to be an arts bookshop, it can be relied on to have something you've never seen before but just can't resist.

117-119 Clerkenwell Road, EC1R 5BY
Tel: 020 7242 9503
Mon-Sat: 10am-7pm

Other branches
➤ 29 Shorts Gardens, WC2H 9AP

MARBY & ELM

If the mot juste eludes you, this little shop may have it. Letterpress printed items for every occasion, from celebrations to good riddance (there's quite a bit of swearing), all printed in-house in vibrant colours: cards, sticking tape, notepads, even jewellery. And if nothing appeals, custom orders are welcome.

53 Exmouth Market, EC1R 4QL
Tel: 07903 419 661
Mon-Sat: 11am-7pm

MARGARET HOWELL

The understated flagship of this famously understated British designer. Ethically-made modern classics don't come cheap, but are made to feel like a worthwhile investment in this light-filled shop, displayed alongside a careful selection of books and furniture and household items from similarly beloved British manufacturers and designers.

34 Wigmore Street, W1U 2RS
Tel: 020 7009 9009
Mon-Wed: 10am-6pm; Thu: 10am-7pm;
Fri & Sat: 10am-6pm; Sun: 12noon-5pm

MHL

Despite being a little lighter on the wallet, it would be crass to call MHL Margaret Howell's diffusion line. Rather it's her workwear-inspired everyday collection: dungarees, raincoats, jackets, airtex shirts. It's pared-down, classic clothing that still manages to look contemporary, presented in an environment as coolly functional as the clothes themselves, just a few paces from some of Shoreditch's glitziest boutiques.

19 Old Nichol Street, E2 7HR
Tel: 020 7033 9494
Mon-Fri: 11am-7pm; Sat: 10am-7pm; Sun 12noon-5pm

MILAGROS

Just as the variety and subtlety of Mexican food is now beginning to be appreciated in this country, the husband and wife team who run this attractive little shop want the same for the country's homewares. There are brightly coloured baskets, glassware, folk art figures, papercuts, and above all handmade tiles, available from stock or as custom orders, that bring sunshine to bathrooms, kitchens and, increasingly, hotels and restaurants across the land.

61 Columbia Road, E2 7RG
Tel: 020 7613 0876
Sat: 12noon-5pm; Sun: 9am-4pm

MINAMOTO KITCHOAN

The only London outpost of a Japanese chain specialising in perfectly packaged Japanese sweets (wagashi) and cakes. They're made with unrefined sugar and very little animal fat, so less bad for you than most Western sweets – and they're rather prettier too, so pretty that this little shop can be quite overrun with people looking at plastic display versions of their items.

44 Piccadilly, W1J 0DS
Tel: 020 7437 3135
Mon-Sat: 10am-8pm; Sun: 10am-7pm

For all your zakka needs
➹ Jasper Morrison, p95
➹ JP Books, p97
➹ Native & Co, p109

MOMOSAN

An exquisite selection of lifestyle and home objects gathered from around the world. Quality of manufacture and design is essential, bringing some cohesion to goods as diverse as Austrian spinning tops, Finnish clogs and wabi-sabi Japanese ceramics.

79a Wilton Way, E8 1BG
Tel: 020 7249 4989
Thu-Sun: 11am-6pm

MOOMIN SHOP

It seems only right that it takes a little hunting to track down a Moomin. In this case, Tove Jansson's elusive creations are tucked away in a small shop in the piazza, which is only accessible via a staircase. Inside is Moomin-branded everything: toys, crockery, soap, snowglobes, clothing, linen and books.

43 Covent Garden Market, WC2E 8RF
Tel: 020 7240 7057
Mon-Sat: 10am-8pm; Sun: 10am-7pm

MOUKI MOU

A small shopfront leads down to a series of rooms filled with a range of lifestyle goods and women's clothing from companies rarely seen in the UK: Rachel Comey, arts & science, 45RPM, DS & Durga, Coral & Tusk. Helpful assistants are keen to help and encourage deeper exploration of this warren-like store.

29 Chiltern Street, W1U 7PL
Tel: 020 7224 4010
Mon-Fri: 11am-7pm; Sat: 10am-6pm; Sun: 12noon-5pm

MR CAD

Just as records and books have survived in a digital world, so too film cameras have their adherents, old and new. For anyone exploring the world of shooting and developing film, this Pimlico shop, packed with secondhand film cameras, equipment, lenses, projectors, lights, darkroom equipment, is essential. Expert staff are on hand to help and repairs undertaken.

12 Upper Tachbrook Street, SW1V 1SH
Tel: 020 8684 8282
Mon-Fri : 10am-5.30pm; Sat: 10am-4pm

Other branches
➻ 41 Carnaby Street, W1F 7DX
➻ 6-17 Tottenham Court Road, W1T 1BF
➻ 157 Kensington High Street, W8 6SU
➻ 37-38 Long Acre, WC2E 9JT
➻ 21 Parkfield Street, N1 0PS
➻ 118/118a Kings Road, SW3 4TR

MUJI

What would we do without Muji? Stationery, toiletries, clothing, bedding, cookware, travel items, toys, furniture and electrical goods are just part of the Japanese retailer's huge range, much of it made in Japan by small manufacturers. Simple, affordable and unfussy in design, all of their unbranded goods have a clear purpose and, since they've been subjected to rigorous testing, they really work. There are a handful of branches across town, but for the greatest variety, this is best.

187 Oxford Street, W1D 2JY
Tel: 020 7437 7503
Mon-Wed: 10am-8pm; Thu: 10am-9pm; Fri & Sat: 10am-8pm; Sun: 12noon-6pm

NATIONAL THEATRE BOOKSHOP

Mining the rich seam of what's on at the National Theatre, the buildings of the Southbank Centre and the surrounding city, this shop presents a changing mix of titles that includes scripts, theatrical history and craft, architecture and guidebooks.

Complementing that is a range of gifts, stationery, cards and posters, including historic NT productions.

Ground Floor Foyer, South Bank, SE1 9PX
Tel: 020 7452 3456
Mon-Sat: 9.30am-10.45pm; Sun: 12noon-6pm

NATIVE & CO

Starkly beautiful Japan and Taiwan-made items such as straw baskets, tool bags, incense, brushes, tenugui towels, ginger graters, slippers, copper canisters and bowls are showcased in this simple, quiet shop. Contemporary and traditional items sit side by side, all showing a shared respect for craft and materials.

116 Kensington Park Road, W11 2PW
Tel: 020 7243 0418
Mon-Sat: 11am-6.30pm

NOOK

Stoke Newington is well supplied with nice shops selling interesting things, most pleasant of all is this one. It's all in the buying – an impeccable selection of stationery, homewares, candles, soaps, books and magazines – and tempting, browseable displays.

153 Stoke Newington Church Street, N16 0UH
Tel: 020 7249 9436
Mon-Sat: 10am-6pm; Sun: 11am-6pm

OI POLLOI

The first London branch for the esteemed Mancunian menswear retailers. Their mixing of classic styles with a contemporary swagger has been copied across the land, but no one does it better. From hats to shoes, and everything in between, the selections are spot on, made all the better by amiable service from genuine enthusiasts.

1 Marshall Street, W1F 9BA
Tel: 020 7734 2585
Mon-Wed: 10am-7pm; Thu: 10am-8pm;
Fri: 10am-7pm; Sun: 11am-5pm

PAUL SMITH

Sporting a cheery green fascia, the focal point of a dark, atmospheric spot within shouting distance of Borough Market, this is one of the smaller outlets in a retail empire that stretches from Nottingham to Nagasaki. It's a narrow little shop with creaky wood floors and worn display cases, an environment well suited to casual pieces from the men's and women's collections alongside books and curiosities that showcase Paul Smith's magpie eye to great effect.

13 Park Street, SE1 9AB
Tel: 020 7403 1678
Mon-Thu: 10am-6pm; Fri: 10am-6.30pm; Sat: 9.30am-6pm

PENTREATH & HALL

A fragrant and eclectic range of items for the home, housed in a delightful Georgian shop – its sign a burst of colour against the black painted exterior. Cushions, candles, books, prints, furniture, lighting and antiques are all part of a mix that favours pattern and colour.

17 Rugby Street, WC1N 3QT
Tel: 020 7430 2526
Mon-Sat: 11am-6pm

PERSEPHONE BOOKS

Headquarters of the small press that reprints neglected works by mid-20th century (mostly) women writers. It is a civilised, tasteful and noble operation, with a shop to match. All of Persephone's books are available, their signature plain grey covers hiding colourful endpapers that use patterns from fabric carefully selected as era-appropriate for each book.

59 Lamb's Conduit Street, WC1N 3NB
Tel: 020 7242 9292
Mon-Fri: 10am-6pm; Sat: 12noon-5pm

PLEASURES OF PAST TIMES

To call this a bookshop would be a disservice. It's a pop culture cornucopia, filled with ephemera to excite and delight: James Bond Batman and The Beatles are all here, as is William Burroughs, pop art, punk rock and shop poodle, Louis.

11 Cecil Court, WC2N 4EZ
Tel: 020 7836 1142
Tue-Fri: 11am-6pm; Sat: 12noon-6pm

PRESENT & CORRECT

On a secluded little street behind Sadlers Wells, this is a place for anyone whose pulse quickens at a glimpse of graph paper or breaks a sweat at the thought of a slide rule. In its displays this stationery and paper goods boutique shows a designer's love of order and colour, while the sheer variety of pens, pencils, paper, tape, pins and rulers – including vintage items as well as new – reveal an enthusiasm for office supplies that can't be faked.

23 Arlington Way, EC1R 1UY
Tel: 020 7278 2460
Tue-Sat: 12noon-6.30pm

RAY STITCH

An excellent sewing shop that meets the requirements of anyone who makes or repairs garments. A wide range of fabrics – including Japanese cottons and Liberty prints – buttons, trims and tools; plus a selection of patterns from big names such as McCall's and Vogue and smaller companies including Merchant and Mills, Colette, Tilly And The Buttons. Sewing classes cover everything from beginners through to specialist techniques. And if all this seems too confusing, staff are on hand to help.

66-68 Essex Road, N1 8LR
Tel: 020 7704 1060
Mon: 10am-4pm; Tue-Sat: 10am-6.30pm; Sun: 11am-5pm

RETROMANIA

There aren't many charity shops where the racks are filled with Dior, Kenzo, Chanel and Yves Saint Laurent, but this is where FARA send all their best stuff – designer items, vintage pieces, accessories and a selection of bric a brac – so the odds of a good score are stacked in your favour. Prices can be high for a charity shop, so just remember that it all goes to a good cause.

6 Upper Tachbrook Street, SW1V 1SH
Tel: 020 7630 7406
Daily: 10am-6pm

Other branches
➼ 130 Talbot Road, W11 1JA

ROUGH TRADE EAST

This is the record shop-as-hangout writ large, with listening posts, live performances and an in-house café and bookshop. As for the music, there's impressive scope, encompassing new releases and scholarly reissues. The Portobello location is smaller, scruffier, and some argue a little more charming for it.

The Old Truman Brewery, 91 Brick Lane, E1 6QL
Tel: 020 7392 7788
Mon-Thu: 9am-9pm; Fri: 9am-8pm;
Sat: 10am-8pm; Sun: 11am-7pm

SCP EAST

Modern and classic furniture and decorative items including chairs by Thonet and Eames, Nelson lamps, Saarinen tables. There's also a good selection of smaller items that make it a good place when looking for a gift: minimalist Braun clocks, tough Puebco tote bags, even chocolate bars and greetings cards.

135-139 Curtain Road, EC2A 3BX
Tel: 020 7739 1869
Mon-Sat: 9.30am-6pm; Sun: 11am-5pm

SHEPHERDS

Start a one-man war on the publishing industry: sign up to one of Shepherds' bookbinding courses, stock up on supplies and soon you'll have the wherewithal to build a library of your own work. If that's a little ambitious, they also undertake custom bookbinding and stock a range of papers, card and writing instruments.

30 Gillingham Street, SW1V 1HU
Tel: 020 7233 9999
Mon-Fri: 10am-6pm; Sat: 10am-5pm

SKANDIUM

In 1999 when Skandium opened their first small shop down the road in Wigmore Street, the Nordic countries' design pedigree had been largely forgotten. Now that aesthetic has filtered back into the mainstream, clever buying means that items and colourways rarely seen elsewhere are still available here – from oven gloves and candlesticks to sofas, lamps and rugs – seductively arranged over two floors.

86 Marylebone High Street, W1U 4QS
Tel: 020 7935 2077
Mon-Wed: 10am-6.30pm; Thu: 10am-7pm;
Fri-Sat: 10am-6.30pm; Sun 11am-5pm

SON OF A STAG

Stocking items from makers including Levi's, Lee, Edwin, Raleigh and Studio D'Artisan, at first glance this shop is barely distinguishable from any number of retailers with a 'heritage' bent, but their range is excellent and staff particularly helpful. Also of note is their alterations service; using their vintage machine they'll chain-stitch any pair of jeans, producing the puckering effect that no ordinary sewing machine can achieve.

9 Dray Walk, E1 6QL
Tel: 020 7247 3333
Mon-Tue: 10am-7pm; Wed: 10.30am-7.30pm;
Thu: 10.30am-8pm; Fri: 10.30am-7.30pm;
Sat: 10.30am-7pm; Sun: 11am-6pm

SOUNDS OF THE UNIVERSE

The retail wing of veteran reissue label Soul Jazz, whose name says much about the stock held in this shop, but not the full story. There's soul, jazz, reggae and funk but also punk, latin, electronic and much more. It's an eclectic selection on vinyl and CD, augmented by their own book imprint and a good used section.

7 Broadwick Street, W1F 0DA
Tel: 020 7734 3430
Mon-Sat: 11am-7.30pm; Sun: 11.30am-5.30pm

SOUNDS THAT SWING

An independent record shop specialising in
rock'n'roll and R&B from the 1950s and 1960s,
with some concessions to later eras. Shelves
are amply stocked with LPs, CDs, stacks of
45s and decorated with memorabilia and
curiosities. With such specialism and the staff's
own penchant for absolutely the most obscure
records, it would be easy for shoppers to feel
excluded, but the reality is quite the opposite.

88 Parkway, NW1 7AN
Tel: 020 7267 4682
Mon-Sat: 11am-6pm; Sun: 12noon-6pm

STANFORDS

The traveller is well served by this great
institution, which has occupied the same
substantial building for over 100 years. Time
marches on, borders change, empires rise and
fall, all of which is documented in the globes,
atlases, travel literature, journals and guides
(including our own) that are stacked from
basement to rafters. Whether you're negotiating
the Orinoco or just fancy a weekend in Lyme
Regis, this is the place to begin your research.

12-14 Long Acre, WC2E 9LP
Tel: 020 7836 1321
Mon-Sat: 9am-8pm; Sun: 11.30am-6pm

Other branches
➻ 23 Kensington Park Road, W11 2EU
➻ 21a Jermyn Street, SW1Y 6LT
➻ 5 & 7 Redchurch Street, E2 7DJ
➻ 40 Old Compton Street, W1D 4TU

SUNSPEL

Clean, simple and, it must be said, somewhat expensive basics for men and women. But think of them as an investment; their logo-free sweatshirts, polo shirts, tees, underwear, knitwear and accessories are all well cut and made to last.

11 (women's) & 13-15 (men's) Chiltern Street, W1U 7PG
Tel: 020 7009 0650
Mon-Sat: 11am-7pm (women's) / 10am-6pm (men's); Sun: 12noon-5pm

TABIO

This Japanese sock maker can be relied upon for all men's and women's hosiery needs. Their range is wide, with classic colours and styles alongside more idiosyncratic offerings. And for just £3 they'll monogram your socks in 15 minutes.

66 Neal Street, WC2H 9PA
Tel: 020 7836 3713
Mon-Sat: 10.30am-7pm; Sun: 12noon-6pm

TI PI TIN

An esoteric selection of independent, self-published and small press art and design books, magazines and artist's monographs. It's a selection you'll struggle to find elsewhere, and at remarkably fair prices too. See their website (tipitin.com) for news of talks and events.

47 Stoke Newington High Street, N16 8EL
No phone
Wed-Fri: 12pm-7pm; Sat: 11am-6pm; Sun: 12pm-6pm

TRAVELLING THROUGH

When the allure of London fades, head to this little bookshop to plan a trip, or at least read about one. Travel is the focus, with guides and memoirs filed alongside fiction, all arranged by location. If escape is out of the question, at least make time to enjoy the café downstairs, with its own small garden.

131 Lower Marsh, SE1 7AE
Tel: 020 7633 9279
Mon-Fri: 9.30am-6.30pm; Sat: 11am-6pm

TURNBULL & ASSER

A showcase for all that's best about classic British menswear. English-made shirts with three-button barrel cuffs (£185); silk ties, scarves and robes, richly patterned in exuberant colours (pocket squares are a more affordable option); luxurious knitwear; over the calf socks in multiple shades; suits, coats and, of course, bespoke options. It's expensive, but looking costs nothing and the window displays alone are enough to brighten a dull day.

71-72 Jermyn Street, SW1Y 6PF
Tel: 020 7808 3000
Mon-Fri: 9am-6pm; Sat: 9.30am-6pm

THE VINTAGE SHOWROOM

There's a level of care in both the selection of items and their display that sets this apart from other sellers of vintage clothing. There are some everyday pieces – tweed jackets, cricket sweaters, workwear, waxed cotton jackets – but the emphasis is on the more serious, collector's end of the spectrum, the very best of which is kept in their appointment-only archives in the basement and across town in Ladbroke Grove.

14 Earlham Street, WC2H 9LN
Tel: 020 7836 3964
Mon-Sat: 11.30am-7.30pm; Sun: 12noon-6pm

WARDOUR NEWS

Along with the usual lottery tickets, Mars bars and daily papers are racks of small-press fashion and lifestyle magazines, along with newspapers to gladden the heart of transplants from across the planet.

118-120 Wardour Street, W1F 0TU
Tel: 020 7437 6131
Mon-Fri: 7am-7pm; Sat: 9am-7pm

MARKETS

BERMONDSEY ANTIQUES MARKET

Hardened hunters gather to pick through dealers' wares as the sun comes up, and anyone wishing to see this market in full flow is advised to follow suit. There are items for most budgets and tastes, silverware, advertising ephemera, glassware, lamps, jewellery and creepy dolls. Despite new, tall blocks of flats on the square that have done nothing to improve the atmosphere, and can make it exceptionally blustery, the market seems in rude health.

Bermondsey Square, SE1 3UN
Fri: 6am-2pm

BOROUGH MARKET

More Borough Market highlights
➤➤ Donuts from Bread Ahead
➤➤ Sausage rolls from Ginger Pig
➤➤ Raclette from Kappacasein
➤➤ Scotch eggs from Scotchtails

Probably the largest gathering of food producers in the country, and arguably the best too. Fresh fruit and vegetables, meat, game, fish, ales and wine, and outlets representing food from around the world, including the shop and tapas bar of Spanish food importers Brindisa. Alongside foodies seeking rare ingredients, many visitors come just to enjoy samples and eat at the many street food stalls and restaurants. A warning: it can get unbearably busy, go early.

Southwark Street, SE1 1TL
Tel: 020 8691 2429
Mon-Thu: 10am-5pm; Fri: 10am-6pm; Sat: 8am-5pm

BROADWAY MARKET

From the ashes of a traditional fruit and veg market emerged a 21st-century take on the theme, with vintage clothing, books, records and many small designers and makers dipping a toe into retail. Alternatively, just come here to eat, there are street food stalls to tempt even the most jaded palate.

Broadway Market, E8 4PH
Sat: 9am-5pm

COLUMBIA ROAD FLOWER MARKET

On Sunday mornings, this street is filled with activity. Stalls selling plants, flowers, bulbs and seeds attract serious horticulturalists along with others who just want something for the table. It's also when the shops, most of which are shuttered during the week, spring to life.

Columbia Road, E2
Sun: 8am-around 3pm

DRUID STREET MARKET

In railway arches and temporary stalls along this industrial stretch, some of the city's most exciting cooks and producers ply their wares. The St. John Bakery's custard donuts did much to popularise the market (queues for them are still inevitable), now joined by butter-makers & Grant, bakers The Snapery, brewers Anspach & Hobday and many more regulars and guests.

Druid Street, SE1 2HH
Sat: 10am-4pm

LEATHER LANE MARKET

Alongside the staples of the London street trader – clothes and bags, phone accessories, tools, flowers, fruit and veg – food stalls have come to dominate this 400-year-old market, making lunchtimes a crush of workers queuing at specialist stalls, many of which are excellent. Space to enjoy your food is at a premium, so we suggest a short walk to Gray's Inn, one of the city's four Inns of Court (professional associations for lawyers and judges), their large, tranquil gardens, called The Walks, are open to the public from 12noon to 2.30pm.

Leather Lane, EC1N 7TJ
Mon-Fri: 10am-2pm

PORTOBELLO ROAD MARKET

A fruit and veg market all week, on Fridays vintage clothing dealers set up in the area under the Westway, attracting serious collectors, designers, fashion stylists and famous faces, alongside seekers of bargain used clothing. Saturdays are busiest, the entire stretch of the market filled with antiques both genuine and otherwise from decades and centuries past, books, records, ephemera and clothing.

Chepstow Villas to Golborne Road, W11
Fri-Sat: 9am-7pm

SPITALFIELDS ANTIQUE MARKET

There are now gleaming, permanent shops such as Belstaff, Rapha and Albam around the perimeter of what was the old fruit and vegetable market, but inside independent traders set up stalls on their chosen days. Visit on Thursdays for antiques, curios and vintage clothing, and on the first and third Friday of every month for a small but recommended record fair.

Horner Square, EC1 6EW
Mon-Fri: 10am-5pm; Sat: 11am-5pm; Sun: 10am-5pm

SPA TERMINUS

Just a short walk from Druid Street (p126), and another stretch of semi-industrial stretch of repurposed railway arches housing small food and drink makers and suppliers. Most of the businesses here usually sell direct to the trade, so this is an opportunity to see where products are made and who makes them. Highlights are Kernel, widely regarded as one of the country's most innovative breweries; Ice Cream Union are known for experimental and seasonal flavours that never sacrifice flavour for mere novelty; we would buy England Preserves for the packaging alone, but the savoury chutneys and sweet jams have flavour to match their visual appeal. There are also importers of cheese, charcuterie and olives, coffee roasters and wine merchants. Don't expect to sit down for a meal here, for that head for Maltby Street (p44), less than 10 minutes' walk away.

Dockley Road Industrial Estate, Dockley Road, SE16 3SF
Sat: 8.30am-2.30pm

SEE &
DO

2 WILLOW ROAD

Erno Goldfinger built this terrace of three
houses facing Hampstead Heath in 1939,
keeping this – the largest – for himself, living
there until his death in 1987. Controversial at
the time of construction, today it's regarded as a
Modernist classic. The house's uncompromising
modernity is offset by the sunny domesticity of
its interiors and the clutter of a busy life.

2 Willow Road, NW3 1TH
Tel: 020 7435 6166
Wed-Sun: 11am-5pm (between 11am-3pm, tours only)

BARBICAN CENTRE

The early life of this arts centre and residential
housing complex was marked by delay and
controversy, but its Brutalist style is back in
favour, making it a destination in its own right
as well as for the events held there: theatre,
dance, art, film and music. The tropical
conservatory is one of the less visited parts of
the structure, but well worth seeking out for
the unexpected delight of organic matter amid
poured concrete.

Silk Street, EC2Y 8DS
Tel: 020 7638 8891
Mon-Sat: 9am-11pm; Sun: 12noon-11pm
Conservatory, Sun and Bank Holidays: 12noon-5pm

BFI & BFI MEDIATHEQUE

The British Film Institute's four-screen cinema shows classic and contemporary films, mixing, new releases, themed seasons and major retrospectives. It's also home to the Mediatheque, which allows anyone free access to the BFI National Archive, an ever growing library of more than 2,500 titles – feature films, shorts, news, stock footage and TV programmes – much of it extremely rare. Should you hit a wall on Youtube searches for obscure clips and movies, here's where to go.

Belvedere Road, SE1 8XT
Tel: 020 7255 1444
Mediatheque, Tue-Sun: 11am-9pm

BLOOMSBURY BOWLING LANES

With authentic vintage furnishings and signs, this is a fairly effective recreation of a slightly down-at-heel American bowling alley. Its popularity as a nightspot may explain why daytime business is limited and the atmosphere a little subdued, but at least no one will see your gutterballs.

Basement of Tavistock Hotel, Bedford Way, WC1H 9EU
Tel: 020 7183 1979
Sun-Tue: 12noon-12midnight; Wed-Thu: 12noon-late;
Fri-Sat: 12noon-3am

BRITISH LIBRARY

You don't need to be a member to enjoy this institution, you don't even need to be able to read; the shop and cafés are open to all, as are exhibitions. A library card is free and grants the reader access to around 14 million books, which is a deal only a fool would resist. The 1990s building is not a conventional beauty, but the feeling of light and air even on a gloomy day is a remarkable achievement.

96 Euston Road, NW1 2DB
Tel: 033 0333 1144
Mon-Thu: 9.30am-8pm; Fri: 9.30am-6pm; Sat: 9.30am-5pm; Sun: 11am-5pm

BRITISH MUSEUM

Little and often is the best way to approach this gargantuan collection that extends from the Stone Age to the present. The Rosetta Stone, Anglo Saxon finds from Sutton Hoo and Egyptian mummies are perennial favourites, but find time to explore less visited areas, working from the top floor down. A refreshment in The Great Court is essential, filled with light and spectacle even on a dull day.

Great Russell Street, WC1B 3DG
Tel: 020 7323 8299
Sat-Thu: 10am-5.30pm; Fri: 10am-8.30pm

BRUNEI GALLERY

A small gallery run by the University of London's School of Oriental and African Studies. Shows focus on aspects of those cultures studied, with topics as varied as textiles, literature, exploration and immigration. The Japanese roof garden is a peaceful spot to eat a sandwich and watch as university students bustle around the campus below.

SOAS, Thornhaugh Street, WC1H 0XG
Tel: 020 7898 4023
Tue-Wed: 10.30am-5pm; Thu: 10.30am-8pm;
Fri-Sat: 10.30am-5pm

CARTOON MUSEUM

In the backstreets between New Oxford Street and the BritishMuseum, this highly specialist gallery treads the line between kids' stuff, graphic novels and satire. A small permanent display offers a broad take on the country's greats, taking in Hogarth, Dan Dare and Minnie The Minx, supplemented by a variety of temporary exhibitions.

35 Little Russell Street, WC1A 2HH
Tel: 020 7580 8155
Tue-Sun: 10.30am-5.30pm

CHELSEA PHYSIC GARDEN

Like every proper secret garden, this one is reached by walking through a small doorway, beyond which lies another world. On the banks of the Thames, behind high brick walls, this beautiful garden has since 1673 been a centre for research and the conservation of plants, now holding many rare indigenous and overseas specimens. Horticultural knowledge is by no means essential; it has an uncommon charm in its planting, with the iron greenhouses and discreet signs that identify species further adding to its appeal. In addition, for once even thrill-seekers, usually poorly served by displays of flora and fauna, can find something to savour in the carnivorous, poisonous and hallucinogenic specimens. There's a comfortable and excellent café too, perfect for relaxing refreshment in one of London's loveliest spots. Run as a charity, it's well worth the entrance fee.

66 Royal Hospital Road, SW3 4HS
Tel: 020 7352 5646
Winter, Mon-Fri: 10am-3pm
Summer, Mon: 11am-5pm;
Tue-Fri & Sun: 11am-6pm

CLOISTER GARDEN

Part of the Museum of the Order of St John, which tells the story of this ancient religious military order, still working today as the St John Ambulance first aid charity. The enclosed garden is accessed through a gate on St Johns Square, giving a feeling of quiet, calm and space for so central a location. Fragrant herbs and medicinal plants add to an atmosphere already suited to peaceful contemplation.

The Museum of the Order of St John, St John's Gate, St John's Lane, EC1M 4DA
Tel: 020 7324 4005
Oct-Jun, Mon-Sat: 10am-5pm
Jul-Sep, daily: 10am-5pm

CURZON BLOOMSBURY

There was a small outcry when this cinema, sunk into the brutalist hulk of the Brunswick Centre, was taken over by the Curzon chain and its name changed from the Renoir, all of which turned out to be a lot of clamour for nothing. With five screens and a steadfast dedication to foreign language, independents and documentaries, it remains one of the city's most interesting and appealing cinemas.

The Brunswick, WC1N 1AW
Tel: 033 0500 1331

DENNIS SEVERS' HOUSE

A truly eccentric attempt to recreate the history of this large house in Spitalfields, exploring this property through the lives of the fictional family who lived here in the 18th and 19th centuries. Half-eaten food, smoking fires and overheard sounds give the impression that the previous occupants have just left each room as you enter it. There's no attempt at authenticity, and anachronistic touches abound, yet despite this, visitors are utterly transported to a different time. Tours are held in silence, enhancing the strangeness of the experience. Winter and night tours are particularly recommended.

18 Folgate Street, E1 6BX
Tel: 020 7247 4013
Tour times vary, see dennissevershouse.co.uk

DULWICH PICTURE GALLERY

Founded in 1811, this was the world's first purpose-built gallery, but what you see today was entirely rebuilt in the 19th century to designs by Sir John Soane (p158). His use of skylights was a striking innovation and results in a space that's light and airy. The permanent collection is dominated by European Old Masters, while temporary exhibitions are wide-ranging and always interesting: Ravilious;

Norman Rockwell; Hockney prints; Paul Nash.
A charming café and lovely gardens should not
be overlooked.

Gallery Road, SE21 7AD
Tel: 020 8693 5254
Bank Holiday Mon, Tue-Sun: 10am-5pm

ESTORICK COLLECTION

The calm, leafy streets of Canonbury are filled
with elegant Georgian houses most of which are
private homes; here's one of the few that anyone
can visit. It's home to a collection of Italian
modern art amassed by Eric Estorick (1913-93),
an art dealer whose clients included Billy
Wilder and Lauren Bacall. The gallery space
isn't huge, but the pieces are exceptional and
temporary exhibitions focus on a time and place
that's often overlooked. A small café makes use
of the pretty courtyard garden.

While in the area, a stroll along New River
Walk is highly recommended. Running from
Canonbury Road to busy St Paul's Road, it's a
manmade woodland that seems not just from a
different place but also a different time.

39a Canonbury Square, N1 2AN
Tel: 020 7704 9522
Wed-Sat: 11am-6pm; Sun: 12noon-5pm

FASHION AND TEXTILE MUSEUM

There's no permanent collection on display here but temporary exhibits explore fashion in all its variety, with compact, thoughtful shows that have focused on individual designers (Kaffe Fassett, Tommy Nutter, Thea Porter, Timney-Fowler, Anna Sui) and themes such as Riviera Style and 20th-century knitwear. Look out for talks and workshops which make full use of the museum's excellent contacts.

83 Bermondsey Street, SE1 3XF
Tel: 020 7407 8664
Tue-Wed: 11am-6pm; Thu: 11am-8pm; Sat: 11am-6pm; Sun: 11am-5pm

FITZROVIA CHAPEL

An extraordinarily ornate unconsecrated 19th-century chapel, glistening with marble and mosaic and lavishly restored by the same developers who have built around it a new complex of shops, offices and flats. The chapel currently has limited opening hours, with plans afoot for concerts and spoken word events.

Fitzroy Place, 2 Pearson Square, W1T 3BF
Tel: 020 3409 9895
Wed: 1pm-6pm

GARDEN MUSEUM

In the deconsecrated church of St Mary-at-Lambeth, has grown this appealing museum which explores the history of the English garden through a whimsical selection of paintings, objects, packaging and ephemera. Recently renovated, with the addition of interactive displays for children, an airy cafe and a shop, it's still engagingly idiosyncratic. John Tradescant, 16th-century explorer and horticulturalist is buried in the grounds, his tomb surrounded by limes, strawberries and herbs, while up above is the church tower – 131 uneven and narrow steps, only seven people allowed at any one time – for views of Lambeth Bridge and Westminster.

Lambeth Palace Road, SE1 7LB
Tel: 020 7401 8865
Sun-Fri: 10.30am-5pm; Sat: 10.30am-4pm
Closed first Monday each month

From above
More great views of the city
➤ The Monument, p149
➤ Tate Modern, p160
➤ Wellington Arch, p165
➤ Parliament Hill, see Hampstead Heath, p170

GEFFRYE MUSEUM

To walk through 11 rooms that display the dwellings of the English middle class from 1600 to the present is to enjoy a kind of guilt-free voyeurism – you're free to admire or disparage their taste as you wish. The museum is accommodated in almshouses, one of which has been restored to its original state, providing some insight into the conditions of the poor and needy in the 18th and 19th centuries.

136 Kingsland Road, E2 8EA
Tel: 020 7739 9893
Tue-Sun: 10am-5pm

GOD'S OWN JUNKYARD

Bringing a touch of Las Vegas to Walthamstow, a huge collection of neon signs and props, collection of the late Chris Bracey, neon designer whose work appeared in films, fashion shoots and many Soho clubs. Flashing, flickering and pulsating in unreal colour, it's an experience a little like entering a computer game. Nerve-calming tea and coffee is available at the in-house café.

Unit 12, Ravenswood Industrial Estate, Shernhall Street, E17 9HQ
Tel: 020 8521 8066
Fri-Sat: 11am-9pm; Sun: 11am-6pm

GOLDEN LANE POOL

Part of Golden Lane Sport & Fitness, owned by the City of London, this pool can usually be relied on for a peaceful dip. While not huge, it has other charms: recently refurbished, its mid-century styling is now gleaming and fresh, glass on three sides keeps it light and bright and at £5 a swim for an adult, it's exceptional value. Tennis courts and gym are also on site.

Fann Street, EC1Y 0SH
Tel: 020 7250 1464
Mon-Fri: 6am-10pm; Sat-Sun: 8am-6pm

GRANT MUSEUM OF ZOOLOGY

Packing a punch that belies its small size, this is a museum that will linger in the visitor's memory. All manner of creatures are here, some pickled, others stuffed, many as skeletons – like the quagga (one of only seven extant examples of this South African zebra, extinct since 1883). There are jars containing bisected heads, another filled with moles, a dolphin foetus, the skull of a giant Ice Age deer and a collection of brains. A strange and wonderful place.

Rockefeller Building, University College London, 21 University Street, WC1E 6DE
Tel: 020 3108 2052
Mon-Sat: 1pm-5pm

GUILDHALL ART GALLERY

Next to the medieval Guildhall, this 1990s building houses the City of London's art collection, which stretches back from the present day to the 17th century, with a focus on scenes of London life. The Victorian era is particularly well-represented and fascinating in the depictions of industrialisation, urban poverty and the emerging middle class. Beneath the gallery are the remains of a Roman amphitheatre, discovered during the gallery's construction and now open to the public.

Guildhall Yard, EC2V 5AE
Tel: 020 7332 3700
Mon-Sat: 10am-5pm; Sun: 12noon-4pm

HACKNEY CITY FARM

The farm's pigs, goats, chickens and geese contentedly go about their daily business mere seconds away from the roar of Hackney Road, their unflappability a lesson to us all. The farm also offers harried townies a rare opportunity to buy fresh hen, duck and goose eggs, as well as plants and vegetables. The café's fried breakfast is highly regarded.

1a Goldsmiths Row, E2 8QA
Tel: 020 7729 6381
Tue-Sun: 10am-4.30pm

HAYWARD GALLERY

Part of the Southbank centre and one of the best places in the city to see large scale retrospectives and exhibitions. There's space to let works breathe and frequently a sense of humour not always found in major galleries. Currently closed for renovation, it's due to reopen in January 2018.

Southbank Centre, Belvedere Road, SE1 8XX
Tel: 020 7960 4200

HORNIMAN MUSEUM & GARDENS

Those with a taste for the outlandish will find much to enjoy at the Horniman, which sits high on a hill above south London. Among the displays are a selection of wall-mounted dogs' heads, African tribal masks, stuffed animals from tiny bird to gigantic walrus, a totem pole, and a torture chair from the Spanish Inquisition – now confirmed as a replica, although it's quite grisly enough. Visitors of a less morbid disposition may enjoy the collection of musical instruments, an aquarium with seahorses and jellyfish, and a café located in the museum's beautiful conservatory.

100 London Road, Forest Hill, SE23 3PQ
Tel: 020 8699 1872
Daily: 10.30am-5.30pm

JEWISH MUSEUM

Located in a terraced house in Camden Town, the museum's permanent collection focuses on the history, rituals and core beliefs of Judaism, with sections on the Holocaust and the long, often fraught history of Jews in Britain. Temporary exhibitions are notable for uncovering aspects of Jewish experience worldwide and digging into the part played on British cultural life by members of the Jewish community, frequently looking at the work of photographers, designers, tailors and musicians.

Raymond Burton House, 129-131 Albert Street, NW1 7NB
Tel: 020 7284 7384
Sat-Thu: 10am-5pm; Fri: 10am-2pm

LAST TUESDAY SOCIETY

A collection of oddities and curiosities, some of which are for sale, others merely for display. Taxidermy looms large, from relatively innocuous mounted butterflies to a full-grown polar bear. Part museum and part shop, it is an ideal place to visit with jaded friends, or to buy them suitably outré gifts.

11 Mare Street, E8 4RP
Tel: 020 7998 3617
Wed-Sun: 12noon-11pm

LEIGHTON HOUSE MUSEUM

Home and studio of Victorian painter Frederic,
Lord Leighton, who, inspired by travels in
Italy, Spain and the Middle East, created
this wonderful miniature palace in which
to entertain, work and display his taste for
excess. Soaring columns, friezes, a fountain
and, at its heart, the double-height Arab Hall,
decorated in an enormous quantity of 15th and
16th-century tiles from Syria. The house exerts
a powerful spell, not least over close neighbour
Jimmy Page ex of Led Zeppelin, a man with an
acknowledged taste for the decadent.

12 Holland Park Road, W14 8LZ
Tel: 020 7602 3316
Wed-Mon: 10am-5.30pm

THE LISSON GALLERY

Away from the art world hurly-burly of Mayfair
and the East End, this gallery has since 1967
quietly attracted an extraordinary array of talent
– Anish Kapoor, Ai Weiwei, Julian Opie, Sol
LeWitt. Made up of two buildings on a sleepy
street off Edgware Road, it's a space to see big
name shows without the crush.

27 Bell Street, NW1 5BY; 67 Lisson Street, NW1 5DA
Tel: 020 7724 2739
Mon-Fri: 10am-6pm; Sat: 11am-5pm

LONDON ZOO

In recent years much has been done to improve the zoo for both inhabitants and visitors. The largest animals have been shipped out to more spacious pastures, leaving more room and a greater emphasis on appropriate environment for those that remain. Walk-through exhibits in which squirrel monkeys and lemurs conduct the business of their days within reach of the visitor are imaginative and exciting, while Land Of The Lions gets you about as close to a pride of Asiatic lions as any sane person would wish to be.

Outer Circle, Regent's Park, NW1 4RY
Tel: 034 4225 1826
Daily: 10am-6pm

MARSHALL STREET BATHS

Wallow in an elegant 1930s swimming pool, enjoy a sauna or make use of the gym, all without the need for membership, and in a local authority facility. Regular classes mean that the pool can be busy or lanes occupied, see their website for details.

15 Marshall Street, W1F 7EL
Tel: 033 3055 0417
Mon-Fri: 6.30am-10pm; Sat-Sun: 8am-8pm

THE MONUMENT

Completed in 1677 as a memorial to the Great
Fire that destroyed most of London 11 years
earlier, good legs are needed to climb the 311
steps, and a strong stomach to savour the view.
At the top of the 202-feet-high tower one is
exposed to the elements, albeit in an iron cage
added in the mid-19th century to stop suicide
attempts, and the effect can be quite unsettling.

Fish St Hill, EC3R 8AH
No phone
Apr-Sep, Daily: 9.30am-6pm
Oct-Mar, Daily: 9.30am-5.30pm

MUSEUM OF BRANDS, PACKAGING AND ADVERTISING

It's appropriate that the best way to describe
this museum is with an advertising slogan:
it does what it says on the tin. Arranged in
chronological order are original, everyday
branded items from the early days of
industrialisation to the present – sweets, soft
drinks, tinned food, cereal. It's a simple premise
and an effective one that works as social history,
nostalgia and on a purely visual level as a
wonderful display of the art of packaging.

111-117 Lancaster Road, W11 1QT
Tel: 020 7243 9611
Tue-Sat: 10am-6pm; Sun: 11am-5pm

NATURAL HISTORY MUSEUM

London residence of dinosaurs and the poor old dodo, the museum's inventory is reason enough to visit, as is the wonderful building, its surfaces scored with intricate carvings of plants and animals. The largest exhibits attract the crowds, but quiet corners hide wonders, and the Wildlife Garden is a gloriously unlikely outpost of wildish nature in South Ken. Ice-skating outside in winter is a magical experience.

Cromwell Road, SW7 5BD
Tel: 020 7942 5511
Daily: 10am-5.50pm

NOVELTY AUTOMATION

A fabulously eccentric collection of coin-operated automated amusements that bring a surreal quality to classic end-of-the-pier games. Stand in front of the Autofrisk and be patted down by a pair of rubber gloves; sit in the Expressive Photobooth and be prompted to change expression; there's also Divorce, Pet Or Meat and many more, all the creations of Novelty Automation founder Tim Hunkin.

1 Princeton Street, WC1R 4AX
Wed: 11am-6pm; Thu: 12noon-8pm; Fri-Sat: 11am-6pm
First Thursday in month, 12noon-9.30pm; bar, 6pm-9.30pm
Opening daily during school holidays

THE OLD OPERATING THEATRE MUSEUM AND HERB GARRET

Up several flights of steep, narrow steps above St Thomas's Church, are a sequence of tiny, creaky rooms packed with 19th-century medical instruments and apparatus, leading into the old operating theatre. Take the tour to absorb every ghastly detail.

9a St. Thomas Street, SE1 9RY
Tel: 020 7188 2679
Daily: 10.30am-5pm

PHOTOGRAPHER'S GALLERY

When the gallery opened in 1971 (a short walk away in Covent Garden) it was the first in the world to be devoted to photography, and it remains admirably focussed. The current space is new, a bold modern overhaul of a handsome red brick warehouse, with gallery spaces from the first floor up, a comfortable – and very popular – café on the ground floor, and shop and print sales in the basement.

16-18 Ramillies Street, W1F 7LW
Tel: 020 7087 9300
Mon-Wed: 10am-6pm; Thu: 10am-8pm during exhibitions;
Fri & Sat: 10am-6pm; Sun: 11am-6pm

PICTUREHOUSE CENTRAL

The small entrance on Great Windmill Street doesn't prepare you for the scale of this glamorous new cinema, with its vast staircase, cascading pendant lights and café, bar and restaurant (all of which only require a valid cinema ticket if buying alcohol after 9pm). There are seven screens in all, thoughtfully designed with the viewer in mind, meaning clear views and comfortable seats. Membership is pushed hard, it gets you cheaper seats and entrance to yet another bar on the top floor, and without it, evening tickets are a punchy £18.

Corner of Shaftesbury Avenue and Great Windmill Street, W1D 7DH
Tel: 087 1902 5755

POETRY LIBRARY AT SOUTHBANK CENTRE

When just a fragment of poetry gets stuck in your head, come here to find its source; the huge holdings are made all the more useful by being searchable by quote, and with the aim to have every work of poetry published in the UK regardless of format, success rates are high. All are welcome in this peaceful place, but members (it's free to join, bring a current ID with proof of address) have greater access to the rolling stacks containing books and magazines.

Parents are encouraged to bring children, and a
Reading Den is located just outside the library.

Level 5, Blue Side, Royal Festival Hall, SE1 8XX
Tel: 020 7921 0664 / 020 7921 0943
Tue-Sun: 11am-8pm

POLLOCK'S TOY MUSEUM

With its creaky, narrow staircases and small,
interconnecting rooms, visiting Pollock's feels
a bit like being inside one of the dollhouses on
display. It is entirely – blissfully – uncorporate
and out of step with the times, a fact
emphasised by a frisky little dog who greets
visitors at the door. There are toys of all vintages
here: an Egyptian clay mouse from 2000BC
shares a cabinet with early 20th-century wax
dolls, a Falklands War game, Action Man, and
19th-century toy theatres of the type made by
the eponymous Mr Pollock. On the ground floor
there's a shop selling toys, games and books,
from just a few pennies upwards.

1 Scala Street, W1T 2HL
Tel: 020 7636 3452
Mon-Sat: 10am-5pm

POSTAL MUSEUM

Due to open as we go to print, early indications are that this exploration of the postal service as a means of communication will have wide appeal. In a location close to Mount Pleasant, one of the largest sorting offices in the world, for many Londoners the museum's most intriguing aspect will be access to a miniature underground railway that has been off limits to members of the public since its construction 75 years ago.

15-20 Phoenix Place, WC1X 0DA
Tel: 0300 0300 700
Daily: 10am-5pm

PRINCE CHARLES CINEMA

Years of late-night Rocky Horror screenings have given this repertory cinema a reputation for rowdiness – not entirely undeserved and never more so than during their all-nighters. It's not all singalongs though, the programming is broad, mixing new releases, classics and cult films shown where possible on 35mm and 70mm rather than digital.

7 Leicester Place, WC2H 7BY
Tel: 020 7494 3654

REGENT STREET CINEMA

In 1896 the Lumiére brothers' Cinématographe was shown here and today, after almost 40 years of use as a student lecture hall, we can again enjoy the flickering images of the silver screen. Showing films on 16mm and 35mm, as well as digital, programming is varied with repertory screenings, classic double bills, retrospectives and new releases. Arrive early for a drink at the bar.

309 Regent Street, W1B 2UW
Tel: 020 7911 5050

RIBA (ROYAL INSTITUTE OF BRITISH ARCHITECTS)

You don't need to be an architect to make use of this excellent institution, situated midway between the madness of Oxford Circus and the calm of Regent's Park. Within a building of Fascist-meets-Deco appearance is a café and, on the first floor a huge bar and restaurant. The bookshop is an excellent source of architectural monographs, guides and related works.

66 Portland Place, W1B 1AD
Tel: 020 7580 5533
Mon: 8am-5.30pm; Tue: 8am-8pm; Wed-Fri: 8am-5.30pm; Sat: 8am-5pm; Sun: 10am-5pm

ROYAL INSTITUTION

Talks and lectures on the subject of science may remind some of slow ticking clocks at school but this august institution, founded in 1799, presents subjects and speakers that manage to be both erudite and entertaining. Events are held in the old lecture hall, its narrow seats arranged in a steeply ascending semi-circle around the speaker. There's also a café on site and a small museum.

21 Albemarle Street, W1S 4BS
Tel: 020 7409 2992
See rigb.org for events

SAATCHI GALLERY

The whims of Charles Saatchi dictate what you'll see in this enormous gallery of contemporary art and photography, which takes as its focus work by young and international artists. The space is pleasing, making good use of a Georgian building previously occupied by the military. The restaurant, Gallery Mess, is also recommended, but booking ahead is a good idea for weekends and holidays.

Duke of York's HQ, King's Road, SW3 4RY
Tel: 020 7811 3070
Daily: 10am-6pm

SCIENCE MUSEUM

Only a mind with a startling lack of curiosity would be bored here. There's Amy Johnson's Gipsy Moth, in which she made her solo flight from England to Australia in 1930, Stephenson's Rocket locomotive, the world's oldest clock and watch collection and the perennially popular cross-section of a lavatory. Photography exhibitions are often excellent and often relatively quiet.

Exhibition Road, SW7 2DD
Tel: 020 7942 4000
Daily: 10am-6pm

SERPENTINE GALLERIES

Within Kensington Gardens and straddling the Serpentine lake, these two contemporary art galleries punch well above relatively modest size; Grayson Perry, Marina Abramovic, Jake and Dinos Chapman, Wolfgang Tillmans, Jeff Koons, Ellsworth Kelly have all exhibited in recent years. In a project inaugurated by Zaha Hadid in 2000, each year a temporary summer pavilion is erected, designed by an international architect.

Kensington Gardens, W2 3XA (Serpentine Gallery)
West Carriage Drive, W2 2AR (Serpentine Sackler Gallery)
Tel: 020 7402 6075
Tue-Sun: 10am-6pm

SIR JOHN SOANE'S MUSEUM

This house museum hovers near the top of any respectable London must-see list, and for good reason. The home and studio of architect Sir John Soane (1753-1837), who built it to display his collection of architectural models, sculpture, paintings and antiquities. In recent years, rooms long off limits have been opened to the public, including domestic spaces and the Catacombs, and Soane's own arrangement of his collection has for the most part been restored. It's a small museum and space is limited which makes queues a possibility.

13 Lincoln's Inn Fields, WC2A 3BP
Tel: 020 7405 2107
Tue-Sat: 10am-5pm

SPITALFIELDS CITY FARM

Just off Brick Lane, across a small, neglected patch of grass lies this unlikely home of donkeys, goats and chickens, including some fortunate former inmates of battery farms. Gardeners will be delighted to learn that fresh manure is available at modest cost.

Buxton Street, E1 5AR
Tel: 020 7247 8762
Oct-Mar, Tue-Sun: 10am-4pm
Apr-Sep, Tue-Sun: 10am-4.30pm

ST DUNSTAN IN THE EAST

A picturesque ruin in the heart of the City.
Climbing plants creep up the walls and through
the glassless windows of this medieval church,
bombed during World War Two. A fountain
shatters the illusion that this is all nature's work,
but the overall effect is deliciously calming amid
the Square Mile's maelstrom.

St Dunstan's Hill, EC3R 5DD
Daily: 8am-7pm or dusk, whichever is earlier

ST PANCRAS GARDENS & ST PANCRAS OLD CHURCH

The redevelopment of Kings Cross hasn't
touched this little churchyard and gardens. It's
a place to wander and ponder, read tombstones
and maybe nibble a sandwich. Notable features
are the Hardy Tree, an old ash around which
are clustered dozens of gravestones in an
arrangement made by Thomas Hardy when he
was an apprentice architect, and the ancient
church at the heart of the gardens – its precise
age is disputed but fragments have been found
dating to 600AD, justifying its name.

Pancras Road, NW1 1UL
Tel: 020 7974 1693

TATE BRITAIN

The arrival of Tate Modern in 2000 rather eclipsed this, its forebear, with the consequence that it's become a more relaxed place to visit and explore. The permanent Walk Through British Art is a remarkable journey, taking in Constable, Turner, Francis Bacon and Genesis P-Orridge. It's worth noting that a boat service runs between Tate Britain and Modern, from Millbank pier.

Millbank, SW1P 4RG
Tel: 020 7887 8888
Daily: 10am-6pm

TATE MODERN

More a destination than mere cultural institution, its vast spaces are constantly thronged with visitors. Blockbuster exhibitions and the Turbine Hall installations are the big hitters, which means the permanent collection can be less busy. The 10-storey Switch House (opened 2016), adds three new galleries and a panoramic roof terrace that provides wonderful views of the city and beyond.

Bankside, SE1 9TG
Tel: 020 7887 8888
Sun-Thu: 10am-6pm; Fri-Sat: 10am-10pm

TRANSPORT MUSEUM

For the millions who use London's public transport network every day, the idea of paying to learn more about the system may seem a case of adding insult to injury, but even the weariest straphanger should find something to enjoy here. More than just a means of getting around, London's transport network is integral to the identity of the city – its red buses, the tube roundel and map are all visual shorthand for London, and here they're seen from earliest iterations to the present, along with many vehicles (1800s sedan chair, advertisement-covered omnibus, the lamented Routemaster, trains) and archive posters. An excellent shop has reproduction posters and more Mind The Gap merchandise than anyone knew existed.

Covent Garden Piazza, WC2E 7BB
Tel: 020 7565 7298
Sun-Thu: 10am-6pm; Fri: 11am-6pm

On the buses
➻ Hardened fans of mass transit may also want to visit the vehicle depot, opened only a few days a year, see ltmuseum.co.uk for details.

TWO TEMPLE PLACE

One of the consolations of London in winter is that only then is this magnificent late Victorian gothic mansion open to the public. Built for William Waldorf Astor, at the time one of the world's richest men, the expression no expense spared takes on new meaning here: carved mahogany panelling, stained glass, marble and parquet floors, and on the oak staircase carved figures from Robin Hood as newel posts. Most of the year it's used for corporate events and weddings, so make use of the annual exhibition that brings together pieces from museums and gallery collections around the country.

2 Temple Place, WC2R 3BD
Tel: 020 7836 3715
*Jan-Apr, Mon: 10am-4.30pm; Wed: 10am-9pm;
Thu-Sat: 10am-4.30pm; Sun: 11am-4.30pm*

VICTORIA & ALBERT MUSEUM

Grandest and loveliest museum of all, devoted to art and design in all forms. Huge tentpole exhibitions draw the crowds, deservedly so, but the permanent collection is one of the city's great joys. We are always drawn to the Cast Courts which house a collection of immense 19th-century copies of classical sculptures, but wander at leisure, dipping into collections of fashion, photography, sculpture, furniture, textiles and jewellery from across the centuries and around the world.

Cromwell Road, SW7 2RL
Tel: 020 7942 2000
Sat-Thu: 10am-5.45pm; Fri: 10am-10pm

V&A MUSEUM OF CHILDHOOD

Taken out of the hands of the children who cherished, played with or wore them, we detect an undertone of melancholy in this collection of toys, games and clothing. A toy lion, bald from caresses is slumped in a cabinet, glassy-eyed dolls stare blankly, and miniature kitchens seem to be preparation for a lifetime of household drudgery. None of which is to say that this is not a wonderful museum, as appealing to adults as it is to children with a programme of events and talks for all generations.

Cambridge Heath Road, E2 9PA
Tel: 020 8983 5200
Daily: 10am-5.45pm

Take a break
➤➤ The museum's three original 19th-century 'refreshment rooms' with decorative tilework are still in use and a must-see.

WALLACE COLLECTION

The pieces that make up this collection were assembled by the Marquesses of Hertford between 1760 and 1880 and bequeathed to the nation in 1897. These acquisitive aristocrats had a weakness for weaponry and armour, Dutch masters and Classical statues, all displayed in beautiful galleries. Despite the splendour of the surroundings, a visit to the Wallace Collection is a pleasingly intimate experience, far from the conveyor belt feel of better known institutions.

Hertford House, Manchester Square, W1U 3BN
Tel: 020 7563 9500
Daily: 10am-5pm

WELLCOME COLLECTION

The cultural wing of medical research giant the Wellcome Trust. Drugs, sex and death have all figured in exhibitions which are thought-provoking without being overly academic. A permanent display from founder Henry Wellcome's collection is a treat for the ghoulishly-inclined with displays that include a fakir's nail-studded shoes and shrunken head.

183 Euston Road, NW1 2BE
Tel: 020 7611 2222
Tue-Wed: 10am-6pm; Thu: 10am-10pm; Fri-Sat: 10am-6pm; Sun: 11am-6pm

WELLINGTON ARCH

Unlike the better known Marble Arch, this triumphal gateway is open to the public, with two exhibition spaces, and a viewing area, from which to survey nearby Hyde Park and the swirling traffic of Park Lane. Plan for a 10.30am visit which should guarantee a view of the Household Cavalry as they pass through, en route to the Changing of the Guard.

Apsley Way, Hyde Park Corner, W1J 7JZ
Tel: 020 7930 2726
Nov-Mar, Daily: 10am-4pm
Apr-Sep, Daily: 10am-6pm
Oct, Daily: 10am-5pm

WHITE CUBE

The larger of this group's two London galleries, containing three exhibition spaces, auditorium and bookshop. The 1970s building provides a suitably stark backdrop for shows by some of the biggest names in contemporary art.

144-152 Bermondsey Street, SE1 3TQ
Tel: 0207 930 5373
Tue-Sat: 10am-6pm; Sun: 12noon-6pm

Other branches
�>+ 25-26 Masons Yard, SW1Y 6BU

WHITECHAPEL GALLERY

They've been showing challenging art here
since 1901, and continue to do so now. Before
or after sating your aesthetic desires, you may
wish to turn your attention to other senses in
the gallery's very pleasant café.

77-82 Whitechapel High Street, E1 7QX
Tel: 020 7522 7888
Tue-Wed: 11am-6pm; Thu: 11am-9pm; Fri-Sun: 11am-6pm

WILTON'S MUSIC HALL

The world's oldest surviving music hall is not
in the best state of repair. In fact it looks to be
on its last legs, despite this it's still functioning
and playing host to cabaret, comedy and music.
When no events are scheduled the hall itself is
closed, but the atmospheric bars are still open.
Those wishing to learn more about the building
may wish to join the guided tour which takes
place most Mondays. And if you have plans for
a grand party, or indeed any event, it's worth
noting that Wilton's can be hired.

1 Graces Alley, E1 8JB
Tel: 020 7702 2789
Bar, Mon-Fri: 5pm-11pm

PARKS

CAMLEY STREET NATURAL PARK

It's easy to forget how close you are to Kings
Cross Station in this little haven on the edge
of Regent's Canal. Insects, amphibians and
sandwich-eating office workers all hover by the
pond, but it's worth exploring further afield too.

12 Camley Street, N1C 4PW
Winter, Daily: 10am-4pm
Summer, Daily: 10am-5pm

HAMPSTEAD HEATH

Tumbling down from the summit of
Hampstead, one of the city's highest points,
the Heath is London's playground. There are
wild woodland spaces, 25 ponds including
three just for swimming (women's, men's and
mixed), Kenwood House – a stately home with
manicured grounds – and in Parliament Hill,
one of the best vantage points from which to
view the city. To the west is Golders Hill Park, a
more formally laid-out area, with tennis courts,
table tennis, croquet lawn and a small zoo, and
The Hill Garden with a vine-covered pergola
providing views across North London.

Hampstead Lane, Hampstead, NW3
Daily: 24 hours
Golders Hill Park, NW11 7QP
Daily: 7.30am-dusk

HOLLAND PARK

One of central London's more surprising green spaces, with its Japanese garden, ornamental ponds and strutting peacocks. In recent years British Longhorn cattle have been introduced in the summer months to munch through bracken, bramble and nettles and so create the conditions required for a wildflower meadow.

Various entrances including Ilchester Place, W8
Daily: 7.30am-dusk

HYDE PARK & KENSINGTON GARDENS

Walking in these two parks you'll be hard pressed to notice where one ends and the other begins so we list them as one enormous space. For some it's enough to enjoy the atmosphere from a deck chair (available for hire from £1.60), others may wish to explore the many gardens, lakes and sculptures, most famously The Albert Memorial and the Peter Pan Statue, placed in the spot beside the Long Water where Peter lands in JM Barrie's story. Rotten Row, a sand-covered bridleway at the southern edge of Hyde Park is still used by the Household Cavalry to exercise, and commercial stables will hire horses and offer lessons.

Various entrances, W2 2UH
Daily: 5am-12midnight

KEW GARDENS

A keen interest in botany is not needed to enjoy these extensive, beautifully landscaped gardens. In addition to many thousand varieties of plant are palm houses and conservatories, a 164-feet tall Chinese pagoda, a treetop walk that allows visitors a view from woodland canopy and, for those daunted by the scale, a tour by 'land train'. Sometimes overlooked, but quite wonderful in their own right, are the Gardens' two art galleries, one focussing entirely on the work of Victorian botanical painter Marianne North, and the Shirley Sherwood Gallery devoted to early botanical art.

Royal Botanic Gardens, TW9 3AE
Tel: 020 8332 5000
Daily from 10am
Closing times vary throughout year

REGENT'S PARK

With Primrose Hill at its northernmost edge, these 400-odd acres of parkland link the city's inner suburbs to the West End. Terrain from meadows to formal gardens is studded with ponds, fountains, sculptures, sports facilities, an open air theatre, cafes, even London Zoo (p148). This variety is central to the park's enormous appeal; neatly clipped where it needs to be, wild and free where it doesn't, it's as suited to picnickers as it is to wildlife, and those who want to spot it. Seek out the St John's Lodge Gardens, sometimes known as the Secret Garden. Reached via a discreetly marked gate on the park's Inner Circle – it's a secluded spot with shady walkways and romantic cul-de-sacs.

Various entrances, NW1 4NR
Daily: 5am-dusk

ST JAMES'S PARK
The oldest of London's Royal Parks and also the grandest, abutting St James's Palace, Buckingham Palace, the Houses of Parliament, Downing Street and Whitehall. Rivalling the ceremony associated with the nearby palaces is another ritual that's not to be missed: the park's pelican population is fed at 2.30pm every day on Duck Island, on the eastern edge of the lake that runs the length of the park, also home to a delightful folly-like cottage.

Various entrances, SW1A 2BJ
Daily: 5am-12midnight

VICTORIA PARK

Consider this a model for a municipal park, providing well for the diverse community that surrounds it. There are tennis courts, a skate park, fishing lake, decorative gardens and untamed expanses. Among many decorative features are a Chinese pagoda and two nooks that are fragments of the old London Bridge, demolished in the 1830s. It's home too to the Victoria Model Steam Boat Club, active since 1904 and holding events on Sundays at the boating lake from Easter until winter, near to which is the excellent Pavilion Café (Old Ford Road entrance, E9 7DE; 8am-6pm), worth visiting in its own right.

Various entrances, E3 5TB
Tel: 020 8985 5699
Daily: 7am-dusk

INDEX

MARKETS

PARKS

INDEX BY POSTCODE

INDEX BY THEME

Whether you're looking to have a camera repaired, see contemporary art, or just eat breakfast. We have it covered.

Herb Lester Associates

Founded in London in 2010, Herb Lester Associates have brought a fresh voice to the familiar. Their beautifully designed guides sidestep famous landmarks and flash-in-the-pan fads in favour of a more beguiling world just around the next corner.

Carefully researched and highly opinionated, the guides highlight the best of new and old; out of the way bars, overlooked eating places, hidden parks, specialist shops, museums and galleries.

Most guides try to tell the reader everything there is to know about a place, Herb Lester Associates just tell you how to enjoy it.